The God Kind of Faith for Total Prosperity

Revised Edition

by
Jim W. Wahlie

ALEF BET COMMUNICATIONS
New Haven, IN

Picture and cover by:
Yehudah Tangeras & Shmuel Wahli

Distributed by:
Lightburst Ministries
3456 St. John's Road
Lima, Ohio 45804-4019

The God Kind of Faith
for Total Prosperity
ISBN 0-9616488-5-6
Copyright © 1985, 1993 by Jim W. Wahlie
3456 St. John's Road
Lima, Ohio 45804-4019

Published by ALEF BET COMMUNICATIONS
809 Lincoln Hwy W.
New Haven, IN 46774

Printed in the United States of America.

Dedication

I dedicate this book to my loving and supportive wife, Carol Ann Wahlie. Carol and I have proven the reality of the Scriptures and the confessions in this book to build a home of love, joy, peace, prosperity and health. Her time and patience has been beyond value to assist me in writing this book. I daily am very grateful that the Lord has given her to me.

Contents

Foreword

The God Kind of Faith for Total Prosperity was inspired in my heart totally by the Holy Spirit.

This book deals with all facets of the Christian life. To be truly successful as a Christian, the first thing you must do is establish once and for all that the Word of God IS the final authority in any situation you may encounter. After this truth is fully confirmed in your heart, you can then proceed in your walk of faith.

If you want to be successful, not just financially but spiritually, mentally, physically, emotionally and socially, you must learn to meditate and confess daily the Word of the Living God.

The meditations and confessions in this book are good — they manifest Christ; they are acceptable — they produce an agreeable state between you and God; and they are perfect — they completely state the will of God. In one sense, this work is a guide to making acceptable sacrifices upon the altar of your heart as you approach the throne of our God.

The present tense of the scriptures and confessions is to assist you to *acknowledge* every good thing which is in you as you are in Christ. In this sense, this work is comprised of acknowledgment statements of yourself in Christ and what God has ordained for you. *Philemon 1:6 KJV*

The scriptures and prayers in this work pertain to the different situations of life. I believe it will be a blessing to you as you read it and meditate on these selected Words of God.

Conn West
Emblems

The Eagle

"They that wait upon the Lord shall renew their strength. They shall mount up with wings as eagles; they shall run and not be weary; and they shall walk and not faint." Isaiah 40:31

As eagles we work with an aim, not rushing ahead or engaging in frivolous deeds. We wait upon the strength of the Lord to fly above the storms of life. And because our strength is from Him, we are continually renewed so we weary not nor faint.

El Shaddai

The Shield

"Above all, taking the Shield of Faith, wherewith ye shall be able to quench all the fiery darts of the wicked."

Ephesians 6:16

The protection, favor, salvation, truth, and face of God are conveyed in the shield. El Shaddai is our affluence to give, to serve, to win, and to receive the blessings of heaven and earth.

artists credit: Bryon Thompson (eagle art)
Gerry Childs (shield art)

About the Author

Jim Wahlie is president of Conn West Freight Systems Inc., Wahlie's Custom Car Care, and Eagle Air Express, in Lima, Ohio. He is the founder and director of Lightburst Ministries. At New Hope Christian Center, he serves as Minister of Music and Trustee/Elder. Jim also is Chairman of the Board of Govenors of the Association of Christian Truckers. His preparation for Christian ministry includes training at Word of Faith Training Center and through the E. W. Kenyon Advanced Bible Course. In his ministry, Jim has taught in Full Gospel Business Men's gatherings as well as in a variety of churches and in numerous home Bible studies.

Jim and his wife, Carol, have one son, David, who is Vice President of Marketing for Conn West. David is married to Beth who assists him at Conn West and works in Data Processing.

This book was inspired by God when He placed a burden in Jim's heart for those people who are sinking beneath the cares of life but do not know how to go about finding the solution to their pressing needs. The reason Jim can speak with such authority on this subject is because he has gone through this same experience in his own life. The answers he found through prayer were revealed to him by the Lord. In this book Jim shares these answers for the benefit of all those in need.

The consensus of this lesson is:

The Lord is always for you;
Satan is always against you.

Matthew 12: 22-30

GOD IS GOOD
SATAN IS BAD

Every good gift comes from our Father. James 1: 16-17

Jesus comes to give abundant life. Satan comes to kill, steal, and destroy. John 10: 10

God anointed Jesus of Nazareth with the Holy Ghost and with power **who went about doing good and healing all** who were oppressed by the devil. Acts 10: 38

For this purpose the Son of God was manifested, **that He might destroy the works of the devil.** I John 3: 8

The blessing of the Lord, it maketh rich and adds no sorrow with it. Prov. 10: 22

Delight thyself in the Lord and **He will give you the desires of your heart.** Commit your ways unto Him and **He will bring it to pass.** Ps. 37: 4,5

1

The Power of the Tongue and the Power in the Word of God

Death and life are in the power of the tongue: and they that love it shall eat the fruit thereof.

Proverbs 18:21

For as (a man) *thinketh in his heart, so is he.*

Proverbs 23:7a

Do you know that you are a product of your thoughts and words? What you are now is a direct result of what you have thought in your heart and expressed with your mouth in the past; because thoughts produce words, and words produce reality.

That's why the Lord cautioned Joshua: *This book of the law shall not depart out of thy **mouth**; but thou shall **meditate** therein day and night, that thou mayest observe to do according to all that is written therein: for **then** thou shalt make thy way **prosperous**, and **then** thou shall have **good success** (Josh. 1:8).*

This verse emphasizes that the way to prosperity and success is to meditate (think, ponder, "mutter" on) the Word of God continually—day and night—being careful to put it into effect. If a person ever expects the Word of God to become reality in his own individual life, he must follow this established pattern of meditation, confession and action. He said in Matthew 6:33, *But seek ye first the kingdom of God, and his righteousness; and all these things shall be added to you.* Put Him first in everything you do then all these things, whatever you want or need, will be added unto you!

In His Word, God has made many promises to His children. As Christians, all those promises are ours, but their fulfillment is not automatic. They are *potentially* ours, but they must be individually appropriated **by faith**. You will receive the fulfillment of God's promises to you personally to the degree that you personally put them first in your mouth, then in your heart - as you meditate and confess them daily (always being careful to act upon what you have thought and said).

That's why this book was written—to help you to learn to appropriate the promises of God through meditation and confession of His Word in faith.

But what is faith? According to Hebrews 11:1, *...faith is the substance of things hoped for, the evidence of things not seen. The Living Bible* paraphrases this verse like this: *What is faith? It is the **confident assurance** that something we want is going to happen. It is the **certainty** that what we hope for is waiting for us, even though we cannot see it up ahead.* So then faith is simply believing that whatever God has promised is actually going to come to pass. That's why the sixth verse of that chapter goes on to tell us that *without faith it is impossible to please him: for he that cometh to God must **believe** that he is, and that he is a rewarder of them that diligently seek him.* If we are to please God, we must believe Him.

But how can a person believe what he cannot see? Where does one get this faith? The answer is found in Romans 10:17: *So then faith cometh by hearing, and hearing by the word of God.* Which simply means that a person can believe something is going to happen even if he does not see it himself, IF he knows that God has said it will come to pass. Second Corinthians 1:20 tells us: *For **all the promises** of God in (Christ) are yea, and in him Amen, unto the glory of God by us.* In the Person of Jesus

Christ, every promise of God finds its yes and its amen (so be it!). And the promises of God are found in His written Word. That's why God commanded Joshua to "meditate therein day and night," because He knew that in it lie the answers and solutions to all of life's problems and situations.

If you want to be successful and prosperous in life—spiritually, mentally, physically, emotionally, socially and financially—you must learn to meditate and confess daily the Word of the Living Lord.

In Mark 11:12-14, 20-26, Jesus gave His disciples a lesson in applied faith, using a miracle He had just performed before their very eyes as an example:

And on the next day, when they were come from Bethany, he was hungry:

And seeing a fig tree afar off having leaves, he came, if haply he might find any thing thereon: and when he came to it, he found nothing but leaves; for the time of figs was not yet.

And Jesus answered and said unto it, No man eat fruit of thee hereafter forever. And his disciples heard it.

And in the morning, as they passed by, they saw the fig tree dried up from the roots.

And Peter calling to remembrance saith unto him, Master, behold, the fig tree which thou cursedst is withered away.

And Jesus answering saith unto them, Have faith in God.

For verily I say unto you, That whosoever shall say unto this mountain, Be thou removed, and be thou cast into the sea; and shall not doubt in his heart, but shall believe that those things which he saith shall come to pass; he shall have whatsoever he saith.

Therefore I say unto you, What things soever ye desire, when ye pray, believe that ye receive them, and ye shall have them.

*And when ye stand praying, forgive, if ye have **ought** against any: that your Father also which is in heaven may forgive you your trespasses.*

But if ye do not forgive, neither will your Father which is in heaven forgive your trespasses.

Jesus told His disciples to "Have faith in God." The center notes in the *King James Version* adds, "Or **have the faith of God or have the God-kind of faith**." Does God have faith? Yes. Notice what He says about His spoken Word in Isaiah 55:10-11:

For as the rain cometh down, and the snow from heaven, and returneth not thither, but watereth the earth, and maketh it bring forth and bud, that it may give seed to the sower, and bread to the eater:

So shall my word be that goeth forth out of my mouth: it shall not return to me void, but it shall accomplish that which I please, and it shall prosper in the thing whereto I sent it.

God believes that what He says will come to pass!

So should we. Not only should we believe that what *God* says will come to pass, but that what *we* say in accordance with His Word will come to pass. This also works in the negative realm as well as the positive realm: Jesus said you would have what you say. If you don't like what you have, start saying what you want, then you'll have what you want! Notice that in Mark 11:22-24 Jesus taught His disciples to speak to the mountain and to tell it to be removed. He assured them that if they spoke with faith and authority, believing in their hearts without doubting what they said would come to pass, it would be accomplished. Meditating and confessing God's Word is a very important part of causing faith to come so you can believe that what you say will come to pass.

If it seems too far-fetched that you have such power at your disposal, think back to your own salvation experience. How do you know you are saved today? Is it not because at one time or another you "believed in your heart" and so "confessed with your mouth" the Lord Jesus Christ in accordance with Romans 10:8-10:

*But what saith it? The word is nigh thee, even in thy mouth, and in thy heart: that is, **the word of faith**, which we preach;*

*That if thou shalt **confess with thy mouth** the Lord Jesus, and shalt **believe in thine heart** that God hath raised him from the dead, thou shalt be saved.*

For with the heart man believeth unto righteousness; and with the mouth confession is made unto salvation.

If you have never received Jesus as your Lord you can do it right now. Pray this prayer with me.

A Prayer For Salvation

Father, You said in Romans 10:8-10 that if I would confess with my mouth that I would be saved. Jesus, You are now my Lord, and I believe in my heart that God raised Jesus from the dead. I am now saved. Forgive me of all of my past life and sins. Come into my heart and make me brand new. Thank You Lord for saving me.

Now that you have received eternal life by believing in your heart and confessing with your mouth, why then would you find it hard to accept that this is also the way you receive anything else from God? Your belief (faith) and confession (profession of that faith) saved you from sin, caused you to be born again, made you a child of God, translated you from the kingdom of darkness into the glorious kingdom of the Son of God. If it did all that for you, it will accomplish anything else you desire in line with God's Word of promise!

You see, God's Word is incorruptible seed "which liveth and abideth for ever" (1 Pet. 1:23). When you speak God's words, you are planting seeds that will live forever, seeds which will not return to God without having accomplished the thing He desires.

In Mark 4:11-32 we read these words spoken by Jesus:

And He said unto them "Unto you it is given to know the mystery of the kingdom of God: but unto them that are without, all these things are done in parables:

That seeing they may see, and not perceive; and hearing they may hear, and not understand; lest at any time they should be converted, and their sins should be forgiven them."

And He said unto them, "Know ye not this parable? and how then will ye know all parables?

The sower soweth the word. And these are they by the way side, where the word is sown; but when they have heard, Satan cometh immediately, and taketh away the word that was sown in their hearts.

And these are they likewise which are sown on stoney ground; who, when they have heard the word, immediately receive it with gladness;

And have no root in themselves, and so endure but for a time: afterward, when affliction or persecution ariseth for the word's sake, immediately they are offended.

And these are they which are sown among thorns; such as hear the word,

And the cares of this world, and the deceitfulness of riches, and the lusts of other things entering in, choke the word, and it becometh unfruitful.

And these are they which are sown on good ground; such as hear the word, and receive it, and bring forth fruit, some thirtyfold, some sixty, and some an hundred.

And he said unto them, Is a candle brought to be put under a bushel, or under a bed, and not to be set on a candlestick?

For there is nothing hid, which shall not be manifested; neither was anything kept secret, but that it should come abroad.

If any man have ears to hear, let him hear.

And he said unto them, Take heed what ye hear: with what measure ye mete, it shall be measured to you: and unto you that hear shall more be given.

For he that hath, to him shall be given: and he that hath not, from him shall be taken even that which he hath.

And he said, So is the kingdom of God, as if a man should cast seed into the ground;

And should sleep, and rise night and day, and the seed should spring and grow up, he knoweth not how.

For the earth bringeth forth fruit of herself; first the blade, then the ear, after that the full corn in the ear.

But when the fruit is brought forth, immediately he putteth in the sickle, because the harvest is come.

And he said, Whereunto shall we liken the kingdom of God? or with what comparison shall we compare it?

It is like a grain of mustard seed, which, when it is sown in the earth, is less than all the seeds that be in the earth:

But when it is sown, **it groweth up,** and becometh greater than all herbs, and shooteth out great branches; so that the fowls of the air may lodge under the shadow of it.

Did you notice in verse 14 (above) that Satan comes **immediately to steal the word when you hear it. There are five things Satan uses to try and steal the word out** of your heart: **affliction, persecution, the cares of this world, the deceitfulness of riches, and the lust of other things.** These five things choke the word. But when you hear the word on good ground you produce some thirty, some sixty, some hundred fold.

You may not understand how the seed of God's Word grows, but it does. It is not necessary to understand the principle of sowing and reaping to benefit from it. All you have to do is plant the seed in faith and wait in patience, confident that somehow, someday, it will produce fruit. You can go on about your normal activities, sleeping and rising, sleeping and rising, and eventually what you have spoken will come to pass. Your responsibility is to keep the weeds out: affliction, persecution, the cares of this world, the deceitfulness of riches, and the lust of other things.

It is not necessary to SEE the seed under the ground to know that it is growing. In 2 Corinthians 5:7 the Apostle Paul tells us: *(For we walk by faith, not by sight.)* And we have already learned that without faith it is impossible to please God. (Heb. 11:6.)

Jesus told His disciples that they could have whatever they said if they would **believe** in their **heart** and speak forth **without doubt**, adding: *Therefore I say unto you, What things soever ye desire, **when ye pray, believe** that ye receive them, and ye shall have them* (Mark 11:24). The writer of Hebrews exhorts us: *Let us hold fast the profession of our faith without wavering; (for he is faithful that promised)* (Heb. 10:23). So then when we pray, we must pray the thing we *desire* (not the problem), in *faith* (believing what we cannot see), holding fast to our *confession* (our profession of faith) **without wavering**, being confident that "he is faithful that promised." If we will do that, sooner or later we will see our desire fulfilled.

The Apostle Paul reminds us: ...*we look **not** at the things which are **seen**, but at the things which are **not** seen: for the things which are seen are temporal; but the things which are **not seen** are eternal* (2 Cor. 4:18). So faith is believing, then speaking, then acting on what God has said in His Word, rather than believing, speaking and acting on what is seen, felt, heard, tasted or smelled. It is putting faith and confidence in our spiritual senses rather than in our physical senses.

Again let's look at Mark 11:12-14, 20-23

And on the next day, when they were come from Bethany, he was hungry:

And seeing a fig tree afar off having leaves, he came, if haply he might find any thing thereon: and when he came to it, he found nothing but leaves; for the time of figs was not yet.

And Jesus answered and said unto it, No man eat fruit of thee hereafter forever. And his disciples heard it.

And in the morning, as they passed by, they saw the fig tree dried up from the roots.

And Peter calling to remembrance saith unto him, Master, behold, the fig tree which thou cursedst is withered away.

And Jesus answering saith unto them, Have faith in God.

For verily I say unto you, that whosoever shall say unto this mountain, Be thou removed, and be thou cast into the sea; and shall not doubt in his heart, but shall believe that those things which he saith shall come to pass; he shall have whatsoever he saith.

For example, suppose you were sick and in pain. The first thing you would want to do in the natural physical realm would be to moan and complain. But if you were truly spiritual and steadfast on the Word of God, you would resist that temptation. Instead, you would turn to God's eternal Word and see what He has to say about your health. You would begin speaking to the sickness (the mountain), ordering it to remove itself from your body. You would steadfastly refuse to give in to doubt or despair, but would continue to believe in your heart that according to the Word of God you are healed. (Is. 53:5; Matt. 8:17; 1 Pet. 2:24.) You would speak forth the Word of God concerning your healing, confessing that by the stripes of Jesus you were healed, therefore you ARE healed. The more you spoke the Word, the more faith would come. (Rom. 10:17.) The greater and stronger your faith, the more you would act upon God's Word, daring to demonstrate that what has been decreed in the spiritual (eternal) realm will be manifested in the physical (temporal).

You see, faith is the same in every realm. Whether it is spiritual, mental, emotional, physical, social or financial, you must SPEAK to the problem. In 2 Corinthians 4:13 Paul tells us: *We having the same spirit of faith, according as it is written, I believed, and therefore have I spoken; we also believe, and therefore speak.* So in every realm of life we SAY (or speak) what God said, then BELIEVE what God said, then ACT on what God said, because *faith, if it hath not works* (corresponding actions) *is dead...* (James 2:17).

Later on, James points out that the tongue controls the body like a rudder controls a ship. (James 3:4.) He also says that the unbridled tongue sets on fire the whole course of nature. (v. 6.) You can either speak in line with what God says and win in this life, or you can speak the problem or circumstance and lose all the blessings God wants you to have, all the fullness of the abundant life Jesus came to give. (John 10:10.)

In Matthew 12:33-37 our Lord made this statement to the Pharisees concerning human speech:

*Either make the tree good, and his fruit good; or else make the tree corrupt, and his fruit corrupt: **for the tree is known by His fruit.***

*O generation of vipers, how can ye, being evil, speak good things? for out of the **abundance of the heart** the mouth speaketh.*

A good man out of the good treasure of the heart bringeth forth good things: and an evil man out of the evil treasure bringeth forth evil things.

*But I say unto you, **That every idle word that men shall speak, they shall give account thereof in the day of judgment.***

For by thy words thou shalt be justified, and by thy words thou shalt be condemned.

So we see then that what we **CONTINUALLY say is what we will CONTINUALLY receive. By OUR OWN WORDS we will be condemned or justified. Therefore** if we are to live in fullness of health, harmony, peace, prosperity and joy, we must learn to continually speak in line with God's Word.

There are **7 basic principles of faith, prayer and confession** which we must learn to apply if we are to receive all that God has in store for us in this life:

1. Say what God says.

It is very important to say or confess what you believe as long as what you believe agrees with God's Word. To confess means "to speak in agreement with." You cannot speak in agreement with God unless you first know what God has said. Then you get your words into line with His. The prophet Amos asks: *Can two walk together except they be agreed?* (Amos 3:3). Learn to agree with God and you will have no problem seeing your words come true.

21

2. Believe what you say.

If confession is agreeing with God, and if faith is believing God, then it naturally follows that no one can succeed very long if he just mouths God's Word without truly believing it. Because without faith it is impossible to please God. (Heb. 11:6.) So saying what God says is essential, but it is not enough. You must also **believe what you say**. Belief in the heart combined with confession with the mouth results in fulfillment of God's promise.

3. Act in love.

In Galatians 5:6 Paul says that in Christ Jesus nothing really matters ...*but faith which worketh by love.* And Peter warns husbands to love their wives and treat them with honor and respect so that their prayers will not be hindered. (1 Pet. 3:7.) Wives submit to your own husbands as to the Lord. (Eph. 5:22) Then both of you need to walk in agape love according to 1 Cor. 13:4-8 AMP.

In John 13:34 our Lord Jesus said: *A new commandment I give unto you, That ye love one another;* **as I have loved you**, *that ye also love one another.* As Christians, we are thus commmanded to love one another as Christ loved us and gave Himself for us. He became poor that we might become rich, He carried our sickness and disease **so we would not have to,** He gave up His life that we might have life—"life in all its fullness" (John 10:10 *TLB*; Is. 53:4,5; Matt:8:17; 2 Cor. 8:9.)

If you expect to get answers to your prayers, you must learn to love others as Christ did. You can not successfully use the NAME of Jesus if you do not consistently show forth the NATURE of Jesus.

4. When you pray, believe.

We have seen that in Mark 11:23 Jesus told His disciples they could have whatever they spoke in faith, if they did not doubt in their hearts it would come to pass. Then in verse 24 He added: *Therefore I say unto you, What things soever ye desire, when ye pray, believe that ye receive them, and ye shall have them.* This is probably where more Christians fail than in any other aspect of their prayer lives (except for total neglect of prayer). It is not enough to pray; prayer must be accompanied by FAITH. "When ye pray, BELIEVE," having your heart fixed and established on the Word of God.

5. When you pray, forgive.

In the next two verses of that passage in Mark 11, Jesus went on to say about prayer:

And **when ye stand praying, forgive,** *if ye have ought against any: that your Father also which is in heaven may forgive you your trespasses.*

But if ye do not forgive, neither will your Father which is in heaven forgive you your trespasses.

If you want your prayers to be answered, you must forgive those who have offended you, even if they have harmed you badly. Now you may not feel like forgiving. It is not necessary to "feel" forgiveness toward the person who has wronged you; you must simply forgive by faith. Say: "In the Name of Jesus, I forgive So-and-So for what he/she did to me." The feelings will come later. The answer to your prayer will come much quicker!

6. When you pray, hold firm.

Luke tells us that Jesus told a parable to illustrate the fact that "men ought always to pray, and not to faint" (Luke 18:1). Literally, this verse indicates that men should always pray with all manner of prayers and not to quit or give up. Many times people pray but do not STAND FIRM long enough to see their desire come to pass.

The writer of Hebrews exhorts us to be "followers of them who through *faith* and *patience* inherit the promises" (Heb. 6:12). And John the Beloved Apostle tells us:

And this is the confidence that we have in him, that, if we ask any thing according to his will, he heareth us:

And if we know he hears us, whatsoever we ask, we **know** *that we have the petitions that we* **desired** *of him* (1 John 5:14,15).

When you pray, hold on to your request until you see it fulfilled.

7. Pray the answer not the problem.

Notice that John said that we pray the things we *desire* of God; we do not pray the problem. Many people go to God to talk to Him about their problem. The more they talk about it, the bigger it gets. That is not the way to pray "according to His will." We must first go to God's Word and find out what His will is concerning our situation. Then we must go to Him— not to "talk about the problem," or to beg Him to remove it, but rather to receive from Him the answer to the problem. We pray what we DESIRE in accordance to His will. And John tells us that when we do that, we know He hears us, and if we know He hears us then we know our petition is granted!

It is imperative that we pray in line with God's Word, asking God to provide that which He has indicated in His Word is His will for us to have.

In Matthew 6:7,8 our Lord Jesus said:

But when ye pray, use no vain repetitions, (speaking the problem) as the heathen do: for they think they shall be heard for their much speaking.

*Be not therefore like unto them: for **your Father knoweth what things ye have need of, before ye ask him**.*

That brings up an interesting question: If God already knows what we need before we ask Him, then why should we have to ask? **Because God does not act in response to need, but in response to FAITH.** While God loves us and is touched by our need, He moves in accordance to faith. We show faith by asking our heavenly Father for something in accordance with His will (word), then believing that we have received it even before we see it with our natural eyes. (Heb. 11:1; Rom. 8:24, 25.) God is a faith God and we must pray in line with His Word, praying *the thing we desire* (not the problem) and He will confirm His Word.

It is best to start out your day with prayer and worship. Each morning, before the busy activities of the day, begin your prayer time by spending a few moments in praise and worship to the Lord. The Lord gives us an outline for praying. Matthew 6:9-13

After this manner therefore pray ye: Our Father which art in heaven, Hallowed be Thy name.

Thy kingdom come. Thy will be done in earth, as it is in heaven.

Give us this day our daily bread.

And forgive us our debts, as we forgive our debtors.

And lead us not into temptation, but deliver us from evil: For thine is the kingdom, and the power, and the glory, forever. Amen.

To *"hallow His Name"* is to call Him by His names. Calling means to proclaim His position in the heavens, in the earth, and in you.

"Thy Kingdom come" is an acknowledgment that the earth is fully submitted to the complete revelation of God in man. Verify His Kingdom coming to your loved ones, businesses, works, etc. (see page 59)

"Give us our daily bread" prepares us to receive His allotments for us spiritually, physically and financially for each day. Take your needs for the month and break them down to daily needs. Claim your daily bread in Jesus' Name according to John 14:13-14.

"Forgive our trespasses." Ask Him to forgive you of your trespasses or sin, then acknowledge His abundant mercy in your life through which you forgive others also.

"You do not lead us into temptation" verifies His continual deliverance from evil. His hand leads us in life and away from death. Bless His Name, and thank Him for His love!

Speak to Him directly and personally, as you would to your earthly parent or best friend. Tell Him you love Him. Call Him by His Names which indicate His divine nature and character. Here are examples.

Lord God, You are:

YHWH (Jehovah, Ya-hú-weh) **my Eternal; my Creator and Keeper, My Light and my Shield** *(Gen 4:26, Ex 3:15, Is 43:1, 45:5)*

YHWH Adonai (A-don-ai): **my Lord, my Ruler, my Governing Powers, my Bread Provider** *(Is 61:1)*

YHWH Elohim (eh-lo-heem): **my Strength, my All in All** *(Gen 2:7)*

El Shaddai (Ale-Shad-di): **You are the Total Source of my Supply, my Total Provision, my Multi Breasted One** *(Gen 17:1, 43:14; Ps 91:1)*

Jehovah Jireh (Yir-eh): **my Provider, my Accomplisher, You meet all my need according to Your riches in glory by Christ Jesus** *(Gen 22:14, Phil 4:19)*

Jehovah Raphah (Ra-fah): **my Healer** *(Ex 15:26)*

Jehovah Nissi (Nees-see): **my Banner, my Sail, my Miracle Worker** *(Ex 17:15)*

Jehovah MeKaddishkem (Me-Kad-dish-kem): **my Sanctifier** *(Ex 31:13, Lev 20:8, Ezek 20:12)*

Jehovah Shalom (Sha-lom): **my Peace, my Completeness** *(Judges 6:24)*

Jehovah Tsvaot (Tsa-va-ot): **my Lord of Hosts, my Commander, my Assembler** *(I Sam 1:3, Is 5:16)*

Jehovah Elyon (El-yon): **my Most High, my Exalted One** *(Ps 7:17, 97:9)*

Jehovah Rohi (Row-ee): **my Shepherd, I do not want for any good thing.** *(Ps 23:1)*

Jehovah Osenu (O-say-nu): **my Maker, my Appointer** *(Ps 95:6)*

Jehovah Tsidkenu (Tsid-kay-nu): **my Righteousness** *(Jer 23:6, 33:16)*

Jehovah Shammah (Sha-mah): **my Ever-Present One** *(Ezek 48:35, Heb 13:5)*

"Lord Jesus, You are:

THE AUTHOR OF MY SALVATION (Heb. 5:9.)
THE BREAD OF LIFE (John 6:35.)
MY DAY STAR (2 Pet. 1:19.)
MY DAYSPRING (Luke 1:78.)
MY DELIVERER (Rom. 11:26.)

EMMANUEL: GOD WITH ME (Matt. 1:23.)
MY GOOD MASTER (Mark 19:16.)
MY GOOD SHEPHERD (John 10:11.)
MY GOVERNOR (Matt. 2:6.)
MY GREAT HIGH PRIEST (Heb. 4:14.)
THE LION OF THE TRIBE OF JUDAH (Rev. 5:5.)
MY LORD OF GLORY (1 Cor. 2:8.)
MY LORD OF LORDS (Rev. 19:16.)
MY MASTER (Matt. 23:10.)
MY MEDIATOR (1 Tim. 2:5.)
MY MESSIAH (Dan. 9:25.)
MY PRINCE OF PEACE (Is. 9:6.)
MY REDEEMER (Is. 49:26.)
MY SAVIOR (Luke 2:11.)
THE WAY, THE TRUTH, AND THE LIFE (John 14:6.)
THE WORD (John 1:1.)."
MY MIGHTY GOD (Is. 9:6)
THE LAMB OF GOD (John 1:29)
THE PRINCE OF LIFE (Acts 3:15)
MY LORD GOD ALMIGHTY (Gen. 17:1)
SUN OF RIGHTOUSNESS (Mal. 4:2)
MY ADVOCATE (I Jn. 2:1)
MY CHIEF CORNERSTONE (Eph. 2:20)
MY ROCK (Deut. 32:4)
MY KING OF KINGS (Rev. 19:16)
MY APOSTLE AND HIGH PRIEST (Heb. 3:1)
THE AUTHOR AND FINISHER OF MY FAITH (Heb. 12:2)
ALPHA AND OMEGA (Rev. 1:8)

John 14:26 says, *"The comforter, which is the Holy Ghost, whom the Father will send in my name, He shall teach you all things and bring all things to your remembrance whatsoever I have said unto you."*

Thank You, Holy Spirit, You are:

MY COMFORTER
MY COUNSELOR
MY HELPER
MY INTERCESSOR
MY ADVOCATE
MY STRENGTHENER
MY STAND BY

You, who the Father has sent in Jesus' Name, You teach me all things and bring all things to my remembrance whatsoever Jesus has ever said unto me.

PSALM 93

You, Lord, You reign; You are clothed with majesty; You are robed. You have girded Yourself with strength and with power, and the world also is established; it cannot be moved. Your throne is established from old. You are from everlasting. The floods have lifted up, O Lord. The floods have lifted up their voice. The floods lift up the roaring of their waves. But You, Lord, You are on high. You are mightier and more glorious than the noise of many waters. Yes, than the mighty breakers in the waves of the sea.

Your testimonies are very sure. Holiness is in Your house, O Lord, forever. You are holy, most holy, God. Hallelujah.

PSALM 97

You, Lord, You reign; the earth rejoices; and the multitude of isles and coastlands are glad! Clouds and darkness are round about You just like at Sinai; righteousness and justice are the foundation of Your throne.

Fire goes before You and burns up Your adversaries round about. Your lightnings illumine the world; the earth sees and trembles. The hills melt like wax at Your presence, Lord, at the presence of You, Lord of the whole earth.

The heavens declare Your righteousness, and all the peoples of the earth see Your glory. All those who serve graven images, who boast themselves of idols are put to shame. Fall prostrate before the Lord, all you gods.

Zion heard, and was glad, and the daughters of Judah rejoiced in relief because of Your judgments, O Lord. For You, Lord, are high above all the earth; You are exalted far above all gods.

I am the one that loves You, Lord, and I hate evil; You preserve my life because I am Your saint; I am the child of the Most High God; You deliver me out of the hand of the wicked.

Light is sown for me as the uncompromisingly righteous and strewn along my pathway; joy is for me as the upright in heart, the irrepressible joy which comes from the consciousness of Your favor and Your protection.

I rejoice in You, Lord, I am the consistently righteous - upright and in right standing with You, Father - and give thanks at the remembrance of Your holiness all the time. Hallelujah.

PSALM 100

I make joyful noises unto You, Lord; I serve You,

Lord, with gladness; I come before Your presence with singing.

I know that You are the Lord my God. You have made me, not I myself. I am one of Your people, a sheep of Your pasture. I enter into Your gates with thanksgiving and Your courts with praise. I am thankful and grateful unto You, and I bless Your Name.

You are my Lord, and You are good. Your mercy and Your lovingkindness are everlasting, and Your truth endures to all generations.

PSALM 103

I bless You, Lord, O my soul, and all that is within me. I bless Your holy name.

I bless You, Lord, O my soul, and I do not forget any of Your benefits:

You forgive all my iniquities; You heal all my diseases;

You redeem my life from destruction; You crown me with loving kindness and tender mercies;

You satisfy my mouth with good things so that my youth is renewed like the eagle's.

You execute righteousness and judgment for all that are oppressed.

You have made Your ways known unto me and to Moses, Your acts unto the children of Israel.

You are merciful and gracious, slow to anger and plenteous in mercy.

You do not always chide: neither do You keep Your anger forever.

You do not deal with us after our sins, nor reward us according to our iniquities.

For as the heavens are high above the earth, so great is Your mercy toward us that fear You.

As far as the east is from the west, so far have You removed our transgressions from us.

Like a father pities his children, so You pity us that fear You.

You know our frame; You remember that we are dust.

As for man, his days are as grass: as a flower of the field, so he flourishes.

For the wind passes over it, and it is gone; and the place thereof knows it no more.

But Your mercy, Lord, is from everlasting to everlasting upon us that fear You, and Your righteousness unto our children's children;

To such as keep Your covenant, and to us who remember Your commandments to do them.

You have prepared Your throne in the heavens and Your kingdom rules over all.

Bless the Lord, you His angels, that excel in strength, that do His commandments, hearkening unto the voice of His word.

Bless the Lord, all you His hosts, you ministers of His that do His pleasure.

Bless the Lord, all His works in all places of His dominion.

My soul, bless the Lord.

PSALM 104

Praise the Lord, oh my soul. Oh Lord, my God, You are very great; You are clothed with splendor and majesty.

You wrap yourself in light as with a garment; You stretch out the heavens like a tent and lay the beams of

Your upper chambers on their waters. You make the clouds Your chariot and ride on the wings of the wind.

You make the angels Your messengers, flames of fire Your servants.

You set the earth on its foundations; it can never be moved.

You covered it with the deep as with a garment; the waters stood above the mountains. But at Your rebuke the waters fled, at the sound of Your thunder they took to flight; they flowed over the mountains, they went down into the valleys, to the place You assigned for them.

You set a boundary they cannot cross; never again will they cover the earth.

You make springs pour water into the ravines; it flows between the mountains. They give water to all the beasts of the field; the wild donkeys quench their thirst. The birds of the air nest by the waters; they sing among the branches.

You water the mountains from Your upper chambers; the earth is satisfied by the fruit of Your work.

You make grass grow for the cattle, and plants for man to cultivate - You bring forth food from the earth: **joy that gladdens my heart, oil to make my face shine, and bread that sustains my heart.**

Your trees, Lord, are well watered, the cedars of Lebanon that You planted. There the birds make their nests; the stork has its home in the pine trees.

The high mountains belong to the wild goats; the crags are a refuge for the coneys.

The moon marks off the seasons, and the sun knows when to go down.

You bring darkness, it becomes night, and all the beasts of the forest prowl. The lions roar for their prey and seek their food from You. The sun rises, and they steal away; they return and lie down in their dens. Then I go out to my work, to my labor until evening.

How many are Your works, O Lord! In wisdom You made them all; the earth is full of Your creatures.

There is the sea, vast and spacious, teeming with creatures beyond number - living things both large and small. There the ships go to and fro, and the Leviathan, which You formed to frolic there.

These all look to You to give them their food at the proper time. When You give it to them, they gather it up; when You open Your hand, they are satisfied with good things. When You hide Your face, they are terrified; when You take away their breath, they die and return to the dust.

When You send Your Spirit, they are created, and You renew the face of the earth.

May the glory of You, Lord, endure forever; may You rejoice in Your works.

You look at the earth, and it trembles; You touch the mountains, and they smoke.

I sing to You, Lord, all my life; I sing praise to You, my God, as long as I live.

May my meditation be pleasing to You, as I rejoice in You. But may sinners vanish from the earth and the wicked be no more.

Praise the Lord, my soul. Hallelujah.

PSALM 105

I give thanks to You, Lord, I call on Your name; I make known among the nations what You have done. I sing to You, I sing praise to You; I tell of all Your wonderful acts.

***I glory in Your holy name; my heart seeks You, Lord and** rejoices. I look to You, Lord, and Your strength; I seek Your face always.*

I remember the wonders You have done, Your miracles, and the judgments You have pronounced, to the descendants of Abraham Your servant, the sons of Jacob, Your chosen ones.

You are the Lord my God; Your judgments are in all the earth.

You remember Your covenant forever, the word You commanded, for a thousand generations, the covenant You made with Abraham, the oath You swore to Isaac.

You confirmed it to Jacob as a decree, to Israel as an everlasting covenant: "To you I will give the land of Canaan as the portion you will inherit."

When we were but few in number, few indeed, and strangers in it, we wandered from nation to nation, from one kingdom to another. You allowed no one to oppress us; for our sake You rebuked the kings: "Do not touch my anointed ones; do my prophets no harm."

You called down famine on the land and destroyed all their supplies of food; and You sent a man before them - Joseph, sold as a slave.

They bruised his feet with shackles, his neck was put in irons, till what You foretold came to pass, till the word of You, Lord, proved him true.

The king sent and released him, the ruler of the people set him free. He made him master of his household, ruler over all he possessed, to discipline his princes as he pleased and to teach his elders wisdom.

Then Israel entered Egypt; Jacob lived as an alien in the land of Ham.

You, Lord, made our people very fruitful; You made us too numerous for our foes, their hearts were turned to hate us, to conspire against Your servants.

You sent Moses, Your servant, and Aaron, whom You had chosen. They performed Your miraculous signs among them, Your wonders in the land of Ham.

You sent darkness and made the land dark - for had they not rebelled against Your words?

You turned their waters into blood, causing their fish to die.

Their land teemed with frogs, which went up into the bedrooms of their rulers.

You spoke, and there came swarms of flies, and gnats throughout their country.

You turned their rain into hail, with lightning throughout their land;

You struck down their vines and fig trees and shattered the trees of their country.

You spoke, and the locusts came, grasshoppers without number; they ate up every green thing in their land, ate up the produce of their soil.

Then You struck down all the firstborn in their land, the firstfruits of all their manhood.

You brought out Israel, laden with silver and gold, and from among their tribes no one faltered.

Egypt was glad when they left, because the dread of Israel had fallen on them.

You spread out a cloud as a covering, and a fire to give light at night.

They asked, and You brought them quail and satisfied them with the bread of heaven.

You opened the rock, and water gushed out; like a river it flowed in the desert.

For You remembered Your holy promise given to Your servant Abraham.

You brought out Your people with rejoicing, Your chosen ones with shouts of joy; You gave us the lands of the nations, and we fell heir to what others had toiled for - that we might keep Your precepts and observe Your laws.

Hallelujah.

PSALM 111

Praise the name of the Lord. I give praise. I give thanks to You with my whole heart in the counsel of the upright and in the congregation.

Your works, oh Lord, are very great. They are sought out by me because I delight in them. Your work is honorable and glorious. Your righteousness endures forever. You have made Your wonderful works to be remembered. You, Lord, are gracious; You're merciful; You're full of loving compassion.

You have given food and provision to me because I reverently and worshipfully fear You. You always remember Your covenant forever, and the imprint of it is on my heart and mind. You have declared and shown Your people the power of Your works. And You give me the heritage of the nations.

The works of Your hands are absolute truth and justice - faithful and right; and all Your decrees and Your precepts are sure. They are fixed, established and trustworthy. They standfast and are established forever and ever, and are done in absolute truth and uprightness.

You have sent redemption for me and all of Your people. You have commanded Your covenant to be forever. Holy is Your name. The reverent fear and worship of You, Lord, is the beginning of all wisdom and praise. My praise of You, Lord, endures forever.

PSALM 112

Praise the name of the Lord. Hallelujah. I am blessed, happy, and fortunate to be envied because I fear and I worship You, Lord. I delight greatly in Your commandments.

My offspring is mighty upon the earth. I am the generation of the upright, and I am blessed. Prosperity, welfare, riches and honor are in my houses and in my businesses. And my righteousness endures forever.

I am a bright light; I arise in this dark world. I am upright; I am gracious. I am compassionate; I am just; I am in right standing with You, Father. It is well with me because I deal generously. I lend, I conduct my affairs with justice.

I am not moved forever. I am the uncompromisingly righteous. I am upright, in right standing with You, Father. I am in everlasting rememberance. I am not afraid of evil tidings. My heart is firmly fixed, trusting, leaning on, and being confident in You, Lord.

My heart is established; I am steady. I am not afraid, I just wait and see the desire established upon my adversaries. I distribute freely to many ministries, and I give to the poor and the needy. My righteousness, uprightness, and right standing with You, Father, endures forever. My horn is exalted with honor.

The wicked men, they see it and they are grieved. In their anger they gnash with their teeth, and they disappear. But the desires of the wicked perish and come to nothing.

PSALM 113

Praise the name of the Lord. Hallelujah. Praise, you servants of the Lord, praise the name of the Lord. Blessed be the name of the Lord from this time forth and forever more.

From the rising of the sun to the going down of it, from the east to the west, Your name, O Lord, is to be praised. And I praise You, and honor You, and give You glory and honor.

You, Lord, are high above all nations, and Your glory is above the heavens. Who is like unto You, Lord my God; who has His seat on high, who humbles Himself to regard the heavens and the earth!

You, Lord, raise the poor out of the dust, and You lift the needy from the ashes, the ash heap and the dung hill that You may seat them with princes, even with the princes of Your people. You make the barren woman to be a homemaker and a joyful mother of children. Praise the name of the Lord. I praise the name of the Lord.

PSALM 150

I praise You, Lord, I praise You in Your sanctuary. I praise You in the firmament of Your power. I praise You for Your mighty acts. I praise You according to Your excellence.

I praise You with the sound of the trumpets, and I praise You with the psaltery of the harp. I praise You with the timbrel and the dance. I praise You with all the stringed instruments and the organs. I praise You upon the loud symbols, and I praise You with the high sounding symbols. Let everything that hath breath praise the Lord! So I say, "I praise You, my Lord!"

PSALM 23

The Lord, You are my shepherd; I do not have any want, You make me to lie down in green pastures; You lead me beside the still waters. You restore my soul. You lead me in the paths of righteousness for Your name sake.

Yea, though I walk through the valley of the shadow of death, I fear no evil for You are with me, Lord. Your rod and Your staff, they comfort me. You prepare a table before me right in the presence of my enemies. You annoint my head with oil, my cup is running over.

Surely goodness and mercy follow me all the days of my life and I dwell in the house of the Lord forever. Hallelujah.

A Prayer for Corporations, Ministries, Individuals

PSALM 91

I dwell in the secret place of the Most High. I remain stable. I am fixed under the shadow of the Almighty whose power no foe can withstand.

I say of You, Lord, "You are my refuge and my fortress. You are my God. On You I lean, I rely on You. And in You, Lord, I confidently trust."

You deliver me from the snare of the fowler and from the deadly pestilence. You cover me with Your pinions and under Your wings I trust and I find refuge. Your truth and Your faithfulness is a shield and a buckler.

I am not afraid of the terror by night nor the arrow that flies by day, nor the pestilence that stalks in darkness, nor the destruction that lay waste at noon day.

A thousand could fall at one side and ten thousand at the other side, but it never comes near me.

I am only a spectator. I am inaccessible in the secret place of the Most High. I just witness the reward of the wicked.

Because I have made You, Lord, my refuge, and You, the Most High, my dwelling place, there is no evil that befalls me; neither, is there any plague or calamity that comes near my dwelling.

You continually give Your angels charge over me to accompany and defend me and preserve me in all my ways. They bear me up so I don't dash my foot against a

stone. I tread upon the lion and the adder. The young
lion and the serpent, I trample under my feet.

Because I have set my love upon You, Lord;
therefore, You deliver me. You set me on high because I
know and understand Your name. I have personal
knowledge of Your grace, and mercy, and love, and
kindness. And I trust and rely on You knowing that You
never leave me nor forsake me.

I call upon You, Lord; You always answer me. You
are always with me in trouble. You deliver me; You
honor me. With long life, You satisfy me and show me
Your salvation.

PSALM 92

It is good and delightful to give thanks and praise
unto You, Most High God. I show forth Your
loving-kindness in the morning and Your faithfulness
by night. With all the instruments, I give You praise
and glory and honor.

For You, O Lord, have made me glad by Your works.
At the deeds of Your hands, I joyfully sing. Oh, how
great are Your doings, O Lord; Your thoughts are very
deep. Rude men and women know not; neither does
a self-confident fool understand.

But though the wicked spring up like grass and all
evil doers flourish, they are doomed to be destroyed
forever. But You, Lord, You're on high forever. For
behold, Your adversaries, O Lord, for behold, Your
enemies, they perish, and all the evil doers shall be
scattered.

But my horn is the emblem of excessive strength and stately grace. You have exalted me like that of a wild ox. I am anointed with fresh oil. My eyes look upon those who lie in wait for me. My ears hear the evil doers that rise up against me.

I am the uncompromisingly righteous; I flourish like palm trees. I am long lived; I am stately; I am upright; I am useful; I am fruitful. I grow like cedars in Lebanon. I am majestic; I am stable; I am durable; I am incorruptible. I am planted in the house of the Lord our God. I flourish in the courts of our God.

I am growing in grace everyday. I bring forth fruit even in old age. I am full of sap, full of spiritual vitality. I am rich in the verdure (the greenery) of trust, and love, and contentment. I am a living memorial to show and to prove that You, Lord, are upright, and You are faithful to Your promises. You are my rock; there is no unrighteousness in You.

The Power is in the Name of Jesus

When you pray, the power is in the name of Jesus. Here are some scriptures for you to stand on in the first person when you pray and when you come against the enemy.

In Genesis 1:26-28, *And God said, Let us make man in our image, after our likeness: and let them have dominion over the fish of the sea, and over the fowl of the air, and over the cattle, and over all the earth, and over every creeping thing that creepeth upon the earth. So God created man in his own image, in the image of God created he him; male and female created he them. And God blessed them and God said unto them, Be fruitful, and multiply, and replenish the earth, and subdue it: and have dominion over the fish of the* sea, and over the fowl of the air, and over every living thing that moveth upon the earth.

The Law is a spiritual writing to convey the realities of the Spirit through physical representations (Rom 7:12, 14). The areas of our dominion and rule on earth symbolize the greater areas of dominion we have in the Spirit. Fish in the Hebrew language depicts one's potential or goal; the fowl of the air represents angels or messages; cattle refer to concepts and ideas; the earth manifests various forms, and the creeping things indicate our movements and stages of development.

From fish to creeping things there is a logical progression of thought as we confess our potential or goal in Christ to the means to fulfill it. Our potential (fish) is supported by messages of support (fowl) which carry forth ideas (cattle) which in turn become manifested in flesh (earthly form), and then move or become empowered by the Holy Spirit to perform the will of heaven in earth (creeping things).

In the first person confirm your position in God's creation:

I am made in the image and in the likeness of Almighty God; I have dominion over every fish (goal) and over every fowl of the air (mind and voices) and over all cattle (ideas) and over the earth (all forms) and over every creeping thing (body movements). I am perfectly built to be united with my mate and with my Heavenly Father. I am expanding, productive, increasing, and filling the earth. My spirit, soul and body are filled with all good things of the heavens and the earth. In Christ I am in charge. So I believe that I receive dominion over everything, over the fish of the sea, over the fowl of the air, and over every living thing that moveth upon the earth in Jesus name.

In Matthew 21:22 He said, *In all things whatsoever you shall ask in prayer believing you shall receive."* **I**

believe whatsoever I ask in prayer **I always receive.** The reason I receive is according to what Jesus said to do. John 14:12-15 says, *"Verily, verily I say unto you he that believeth on me, the works that I do shall he do also and greater works than these shall he do because I go unto my Father.* **Whatsoever** *you shall ask in my name that will I do that the Father may be glorified in the Son. If you shall ask* **anything in my name, I will do it.** *If you love Me, keep My commandments."* I believe in You, Jesus, and the works that You do, I do. And greater works than these I do because You went back to the Father. And whatsoever I **ask, claim or command,** in Your Name I receive that the Father may be glorified in the Son. When I ask **anything** in Your name You always do it. I love You, and I keep Your commandments.

John 15:7 says, *"If you abide in Me and My words abide in you, you shall ask what you will and it shall be done unto you."* I abide in You and Your words abide in me; I ask whatever I will, and it is done unto me.

John 15:16 says, *"You have not chosen me but I have chosen you and have ordained you to go forth and bring forth fruit and that your fruit should remain, that whatsoever you shall ask of the Father in my name he may give it you."* I thank You, Lord, that You have chosen me and I have chosen You. And You ordained me that I bring forth fruit, and my fruit remains. And whatsoever I **ask** the Father in Your name, Jesus, You give it to me.

John 16:23-24 says, *"In that day you shall ask me nothing. Verily, verily I say unto you whatsoever you shall ask the Father in my name He will give it to you. Hither to, have you ask nothing in my name, ask and you shall receive that your joy may be full."* So I thank You, Father, that whatsoever I ask of You, Father, in Jesus' Name, You always give it to me. I ask and receive that my joy is always full.

Ephesians 1:15-23, *Wherefore I also, after I heard of your faith in the Lord Jesus, and love unto all the saints, Cease not to give thanks for you, making mention of you in my prayers; That the God of our Lord Jesus Christ, the Father of glory, may give unto you the spirit of wisdom and revelation in the knowledge of him: The eyes of your understanding being enlightened; that ye may know what is the hope of his calling, and what the riches of the glory of his inheritance in the saints, And what is the exceeding greatness of his power to us-ward who believe, according to the working of his mighty power, Which he wrought in Christ, when he raised him from the dead, and set him at his own right hand in the heavenly places, Far above all principality, and power, and might, and dominion, and every name that is named, not only in this world, but also in that which is to come: And hath put all things under his feet, and gave him to be the head over all things to the church, Which is his body, the fulness of him that filleth all in all.*

Philippians 2:5-11, *Let this mind be in you, which was also in Christ Jesus: Who, being in the form of God, thought it not robbery to be equal with God: But made himself of no reputation, and took upon him the form of a servant, and was made in the likeness of men: And being found in fashion as a man, he humbled himself, and became obedient unto death, even the death of the cross. Wherefore God also hath highly exalted him, and given him a name which is above every name: That at the name of Jesus every knee should bow, of things in heaven, and things in earth, and things under the earth; And that every tongue should confess that Jesus Christ is Lord, to the glory of God the Father.*

Psalm 138:2, *I will worship toward thy holy temple, and praise thy name for thy loving-kindness and for thy truth:* **for thou has magnified thy word above all thy name.**

After examining these scriptures, you can see that Jesus has been given all authority over all things, and a Name which is above every name. He gave us His Name to use so we can defeat the enemy in every area of our lives. **Glory to God!**

In this book I have included some confessions of faith drawn directly from Scripture, followed by some prayers based on the Word of God.

You should foremost acknowledge every good thing within you to build yourself up, and then to pray for others, the leaders of our country, etc... (1 Tim. 2:1,2.) Pray also for your loved ones and other people whom God has laid on your heart, including ministers and lay people.

If you will continually pray for others and speak forth God's Word for yourself, you will soon have *total prosperity* in this life through Jesus Christ.

God bless you.

Jim W. Wahlie

The LORD Bless You and Keep You ...

The LORD Make His Face Shine Upon You and Be Gracious Unto You ...

The LORD Lift Up His Countenance Upon You and Give You Peace.

2

Prayer for Self

Life and death are in the power of the tongue: and they that love it shall eat the fruit thereof.

Proverbs 18:21

Mark 16:15-20, **And he said unto them, "Go ye into all the world, and preach the gospel to every creature. He that believeth and is baptized shall be saved; but he that believeth not shall be damned. And these signs shall follow them that believe; In my name shall they cast out devils; they shall speak with new tongues; They shall take up serpents; and if they drink any deadly thing, it shall not hurt them; they shall lay hands on the sick, and they shall recover." So then after the Lord had spoken unto them, he was received up into heaven, and sat on the right hand of God. And they went forth, and preached everywhere, the Lord working with them, and confirming the word with signs following. Amen.**

I am a believer, not a doubter, so these signs follow me. In the Name of Jesus I cast out devils; I speak with new tongues; I take up serpents; if I eat or drink any deadly thing it will not harm me; I lay hands on the sick, and they recover. I go forth and preach and teach everywhere. The Lord works with me and confirms His Word with signs following.

Matthew 16:18-19, **And I say also unto thee, That thou art Peter, and upon this rock I will build my church; and the gates of hell shall not prevail against** it. And I will give unto thee the keys of the kingdom of heaven: and whatsoever thou shalt bind on earth shall be bound in heaven: and whatsoever thou shalt loose on earth shall be loosed in heaven.

Matthew 12:28, But if I cast out devils by the Spirit of God then the kingdom of God is come unto you, or else how can one enter into a strong man's house and spoil his goods except he first bind the strong man, and then he will spoil his house.

Lord Jesus, You have given me authority to use Your Name, You who are the head of all principality and power. That which I bind on earth is bound in heaven. Therefore, in the Name of Jesus Christ, I bind all principalities, all powers, all the rulers of the darkness of this world, all the spiritual wickedness in high places.

Satan, in the Name of Jesus, I command you to stop all your maneuvers against me.

Hebrews 1:13-14, But to which of the angels said he at any time, Sit on my right hand, until I make thine enemies thy footstool? Are they not all ministering spirits, sent forth to minister for them who shall be heirs of salvation?

Psalm 103:19-20, The Lord hath prepared his throne in the heavens; and his kingdom ruleth over all. Bless the Lord, ye his angels, that excel in strength, that do his commandments, hearkening unto the voice of his word.

Ministering spirits, I loose you to bring me prosperity - spiritually, mentally, emotionally, physically, socially and financially. Likewise, I loose or release my body unto holy service whereby my mind is also set free to serve God in Christ.

Father, this book of the law does not depart out of my mouth; but I meditate therein day and night, and I observe to do all that is written therein: for then I make my way prosperous, and then I have good success.

Lord, You said that I could have whatever I say, if I believe it in my heart. Your Word is like a seed which I plant in my heart with my mouth. My heart is good ground. That seed is growing and will burst forth into fruit. I have what I say, because I believe it in my heart. Be it unto me according to Thy Word.

Lord, I roll all my works upon You. I commit and trust them wholly to You; [You cause my thoughts to become agreeable to Your will, and] so are my plans established and they succeed. My dreams (ideas) come through a multitude of business. Through wisdom, knowledge and prudence, You give me witty inventions. My home and business are built by wise planning. I am strong through common sense. I profit wonderfully by keeping abreast of the facts. I am made rich in every way so that I am generous on every occasion, and through me Your generosity will result in thanksgiving to You.

Thank You, Father, for giving me *total prosperity* in life through my Lord Jesus Christ! Amen!

Scripture Reference: Josh. 1:8; Mark 11:23,24; 4:30-34; Luke 1:38; Mark 16:15-20; Luke 10:19; Matt. 18:18,19; Col. 2:10; Eph. 6:10-18; Heb. 1:14; Prov. 16:3 AMP; Eccl. 5:3; Prov. 8:12; Prov. 24:3-5 TLB; 2 Cor, 9:11 NIV; John 10:10.

Isaiah 43:1-7, **But now thus saith the Lord that created thee, O Jacob, and he that formed thee, O Israel, Fear not: for I have redeemed thee, I have called thee by thy name; thou art mine. When thou passest through the waters, I will be with thee; and through the rivers,** they shall not overflow thee: when thou walkest through the fire, thou shalt not be burned; neither shall the flame kindle upon thee. For I am the Lord thy God, the Holy One of Israel, thy Saviour: I gave Egypt for thy ransom, Ethiopia and Seba for thee. Since thou wast precious in my sight, thou hast been honorable, and I have loved thee: therefore will I give men for thee, and people for thy life. Fear not: for I am with thee: I will bring thy seed from the east, and gather thee from the west; I will say to the north, Give up; and to the south, Keep not back: bring my sons from far, and my daughters from the ends of the earth; Even every one that is called by my name: for I have created him for my glory, I have formed him; yea, I have made him.

Now I say to the north, south, east and west, Give up; keep not back; turn loose of the things that belong to me in Jesus' Name! Satan is a thief, and he comes to kill, steal and destroy. He is the one that holds everything back from you. Call forth what you need from the north, south, east and west. Then loose your angels to go out and acquire it.

Isaiah 45:11, Thus saith the Lord, the Holy One of Israel, and his Maker, Ask me of things to come concerning my sons, and concerning the work of my hands command ye me.

Ask the Lord to show you things to come concerning your future; believe that He will answer, and He will. I command in Jesus' Name all things on earth appointed for me to be turned loose, and I command these things to come unto me in the name of Jesus. You also can command the demons to flee and the sick to be healed in Jesus' Name (Acts 3:1-16, I Cor. 12:1-12, Rom. 8:14)

Zechariah 4:6-7, **Then he answered and spake unto me, saying, This is the word of the Lord unto Zerubbabel, saying, Not by might, nor by power, but by my spirit, saith the Lord of hosts. Who art thou, O great mountain? before Zerubbabel thou shalt become a plain: and he shall bring forth the headstone thereof with shoutings, crying, Grace, grace unto it.**

Place all your mountains (problems) before the Lord and start shouting Grace, grace unto them in Jesus' Name, and they will become a plain! "It's not by might, nor by power, but by My spirit," saith the Lord of host.

Confessions to Strengthen You in Faith and in Virtue, and Cause You to Never Fall

Grace and peace be multiplied unto you through the knowledge of God, and of Jesus our Lord, According as his divine power hath given unto us all things that pertain unto life and godliness, through the knowledge of him that hath called us to glory and virtue:

Whereby are given unto us exceeding great and precious promises: that by these ye might be partakers of the divine nature, having escaped the corruption that is in the world through lust.

And beside this, giving all diligence, add to your faith virtue; and to virtue knowledge; and to knowledge temperance; and to temperance patience; and to patience godliness; and to godliness brotherly kindness; and to brotherly kindness charity.

*For if these things be in you, and abound, they make you that ye shall neither be barren nor unfruitful in the knowledge of our Lord Jesus Christ. But he that lacketh these things is blind, and cannot see afar off, and hath forgotten that he was purged from his old sins. Wherefore the rather, brethren, give diligence to make your calling and election sure: for if ye do these things, **ye shall never fall.***

2 Peter 1:2-10

My Personal Acknowledgement of Christ Jesus

Grace and peace are multiplied unto me through the knowledge of God, and of Jesus my Lord, according to Your divine power, You have given unto me all things that pertain unto life and godliness, through the knowledge of You that calls me to glory and virtue:

Whereby you have given unto me exceeding great and precious promises: that by these I am a partaker of Your divine nature, having escaped the corruption that is in the world through lust.

And beside this, giving all diligence, I add to my faith virtue; and to my virtue knowledge; and to my knowledge temperance; and to my temperance patience; and to my patience godliness; and to my godliness brotherly kindness; and to my brotherly kindness agape love.

For as these things are in me, and abound, I am neither barren nor unfruitful in the knowledge of my Lord Jesus Christ. I give diligence to make my calling and election sure: for as I do these things, **I never fall.**

God calls those things that be not as though they were.

As it is written, I have made thee a father of many nations, before Him whom he believed, even God, who quickeneth the dead, and calleth those things which be not as though they were. Who against hope believed in hope, that he might become the father of many nations, acccording to that which was spoken, so shall thy seed be.

And being not weak in faith, he considered not his own body now dead, when he was about an hundred years old, neither yet the deadness of Sarah's womb: He staggered not at the promise of God through unbelief; but was strong in faith, giving glory to God; and being fully persuaded that, what He had promised, He was able also to perform.

Rom 4:17-21, KJV

Author's Statement of Faith

I, Jim Wahlie, against hope believe in hope and am not weak in faith. I do not consider circumstances, and I do not stagger at the promises of God through unbelief; but I am strong in faith, giving glory to God.

I am fully persuaded that, what my God has promised, He is able to and WILL perform. I say that God and His Word are true, and I am independent of all circumstances.

I always walk in agape love and think the best of every person. I am slow to speak and quick to forgive. With the help of the Lord I always do good, am rich in good deeds, am generous and willing to share. In this way I lay up treasure for myself as a firm foundation for the coming age, so that I may take hold of the life that is truly life.

Scripture Reference: Rom. 4:17-22; 3:4; Phil. 4:11 TCNT; Eph. 5:2; James 1:19; Mark 11:25; 1 Tim. 6:18,19 NIV

II Timothy 1:12, *For the which cause I also suffer these things: nevertheless I am not ashamed: for I know whom I have believed, and am persuaded that he is able to keep that which I have committed unto him against that day.*

Isaiah 59:19, *So shall they fear the name of the Lord from the west, and his glory from the rising of the sun. When the enemy shall come in, like a flood the Spirit of the Lord shall lift up a standard against him.*

I am not ashamed of the gospel for I know whom I have believed. And I am persuaded that He is able and He will keep that which I have committed unto Him against that day. I am the one that fears the name of the Lord, and I see Your glory from the rising of the sun. When the enemy comes in, like a flood, You, the Spirit of the Lord will raise up a standard against him.

A Virtuous Woman

Who can find a virtuous woman? For my price is far above rubies. The heart of my husband safely trusts in me, so that I have no need of spoil. I will do him good and not evil all the days of my life.

I seek wool, and flax, and work willingly with my hands. I am like the merchant ships; I bring my food from afar. I rise also while it is yet night, and give meat to my household, and a portion to my maidens.

I consider a field, and buy it: with the fruit of my hands I plant a vineyard. I gird my loins with strength, and strengthen my arms. I perceive that my merchandise is good: my candle does not go out at night.

I lay my hands to the spindle, and my hands hold the distaff. I stretch out my hand to the poor; yea, I reach forth my hands to the needy. I am not afraid of the snow for my household: for all my household are clothed with scarlet. I make myself coverings of tapestry; my clothing is silk and purple. My husband is known in the gates, when he sits among the elders of the land.

I make fine linen, and sell it; and deliver girdles unto the merchant. Strength and honour are my clothing; and I shall rejoice in time to come.

I open my mouth with wisdom; and in my tongue is the law of kindness. I look well to the ways of my household, and eat not the bread of idleness.

My children rise up, and call me blessed; my husband also, and he praises me: "Many daughters have done virtuously, but I excel them all."

Favour is deceitful, and beauty is vain: but I am a woman who fears You, Lord, and therefore I am praised. Give me of the fruit of my hands; and let my own works praise me in the gates.

Prov 31:10-31

3
Prayers for Others

And this is the confidence that we have in him, that,
*if we ask any thing **according to his will**, he heareth us:*

And if we know that he hear us, whatsoever we ask,
we know that we have the petitions that we desired of
him.
1 John 5:14,15

A Prayer for Positions

(Heads of States, Leaders of Nations, the President, Vice
President, House of Representatives, Senators, Congress,
Judges, Officers of the Law, Mayors, Lawyers, Governors,
Families, and others.)

In the Name of Jesus Christ, I bind you, Satan,
and I break all your power over the following people.

Heavenly Father, I come to You in Jesus' Name.
I claim _____, _____,
_____, _____,
_____, and _____
into Your kingdom. I say that they are SAVED and
FILLED with the Holy Ghost and are doers of the
Word. The fruit of the Spirit and the gifts of the Spirit
are manifest in our lives all the time!

I claim all of us in fellowship with You, Father.
I thank You that we have the Spirit of wisdom and
revelation knowledge and understanding, that we are
strengthened with all might (ability to perform any
task), and that the eyes of our understanding are

enlightened so we know the hope to which You have called us, the riches of Your glorious inheritance in the saints, and Your incomparable great power for us as believers.

I thank You, Father, that we are rooted and grounded in agape love which is shed abroad in our hearts by the Holy Ghost. I declare that we have the power to comprehend with all the saints the totality of You and that we know the love of Christ which surpasses human knowledge. We are filled to overflowing with Your fullness, Father. We are all led by You, Holy Spirit, and are willing and obedient to Your voice. We obey Your Word. We are all diligent and excellent stewards of everything You have given us.

As Jesus is, so are we in this world! We have the mind of Christ. This is the heritage of the servants of the Lord, and our righteousness is of You, Jesus.

I thank You, Father, that _____ and I are together in marriage in Your perfect will. We are completely one in flesh and spirit. We are led by You, Holy Spirit and are always willing and obedient to Your voice.

All of us live in divine life and are redeemed from the curse of the law.

In Jesus' Name I bind, curse, cut off the lust of the eyes and the lust of the flesh, strife, pride, adultery, fornication, hardness of heart, debt, strong drink, smoking, divorce, abortion, pornography, pollution, uncleanness, theft, selfishness, poverty, lack, want, sickness, disease, fear, worry, doubt, unbelief and every other thing that would come between us and You, Lord, to rob us of our love, joy, peace, prosperity and fellowship with You. I loose prosperity in abundance - spiritually, mentally, emotionally, physically, socially, financially and materially. We are filled to overflowing with **AGAPE LOVE, JOY** and **PEACE** and are continually **PREACHING AND TEACHING THE GOOD NEWS TO ALL PEOPLE.** Our steps are ordered by You, Lord, and You delight in our way.

For all this, I give You thanks in the Name of Jesus. Amen.

Scripture Reference: Matt. 18:18; Mark 3:27; James 1:22; Gal. 5:22,23; Col. 1:11; Eph. 3:16-19; 1:17-19; Rom. 8:14; 1 Cor. 4:1,2; 1 Pet. 4:10; 1 John 4:17; 1 Cor. 2:16; Is. 54:17; 1 Cor. 1:30; Gal. 3:13,14; Ps. 37:23.

A Prayer for the Body of Christ

Father, in the Name of Jesus, I bring before You the body of believers of _____ and those scattered all over the world. I confess with my mouth, through faith in Your Word, that we let no foul or polluting language, nor evil word, nor unwholesome or worthless talk [ever] come out of our mouths, but only such [speech] as is good and beneficial to the spiritual progress of others as it is fitting to the need and the occasion, that it may be a blessing and give grace (Your favor) to those who hear it.

In the Name of Jesus Christ, I curse (cut off) all bitterness, indignation, wrath, (passion, rage, bad temper) resentment, (anger, animosity) quarreling (brawling, clamor, contention) and slander (evil speaking, abusive or blasphemous language); banish it from us. We are useful, helpful and kind to one another, tenderhearted (compassionate, understanding, loving-hearted), forgiving one another (readily and freely), as You in Christ forgive us, we forgive others.

I declare that righteousness is exalted in our nation. I curse (cut off) all unrighteousness in Jesus' Name.

Thank You, Father, that we walk in agape love—esteeming and delighting in one another—as Christ loved us and gave Himself up for us, a slain offering and sacrifice to You. In the Name of Jesus, I say that we continue in prayer, and watch in the same, with thanksgiving, and that our prayers avail much because we have been made righteous and holy through the Lord Jesus Christ.

I thank You, Father, that You watch over Your Word to perform it. I believe that I have received this request, according to Mark 11:23,24. In Jesus' Name, I thank You for it. Amen.

Scripture Reference: Eph. 4:29,31-32 AMP; Prov. 14:34; Eph. 5:1,2 AMP; Col. 4:2; James 5:16; 2 Cor. 5:21; Jer. 1:12 AMP.

A Prayer for Ministers

(Apostles, Prophets, Evangelists, Pastors, Teachers, Missionaries, Bishops, Elders, Deacons, Ushers, Gideons, Musicians, Gospel Singers, Helps)

Father, in the Name of Jesus, I confess that we are men and women who are responsible for giving out Your Gospel. We have been given the spirit of wisdom and revelation in the knowledge of You, the eyes of our understanding having been enlightened, that we know what is the hope of Your calling, and what are the riches of the glory of Your inheritance in the saints, and what is the exceeding greatness of Your power to us who believe.

I thank You, Father, that we continue in prayer, and watch in the same with thanksgiving, that we make the mystery of the Gospel manifest as we ought to speak. I thank You that we know how we ought to answer every man, and we answer every person according to Your Word and the leading of You, Holy Spirit.

Because of faith in Your Word, I say with my mouth that we are *filled* with the knowledge of Your will in all wisdom and spiritual understanding; that we walk worthy of You, Lord, unto all pleasing, being fruitful in every good work, and filled with the knowledge of You, Father, strengthened with all might, according to Your glorious power, unto all patience and longsuffering with joyfulness.

I thank You, Father, that You have made us meet to be partakers of the inheritance of the saints in light, You have delivered us from the power of darkness, and have translated us into the kingdom of Your dear Son; as Jesus is, so are we in this world. We have the mind of Christ and are always in fellowship with You, walking in Your perfect will.

I confess that we speak the truth in love; we have matured in You in all things. Your Word, which we speak, is quick and powerful, and sharper than any twoedged sword, piercing even to the dividing asunder of soul and spirit, and of the joints and marrow, and is a discerner of the thoughts and intents of the heart.

We have an unction from You, Holy Spirit, who knows all things. The anointing which we have received from You abides in us, and we need not that any teach us: but as the same anointing teaches us of all things, and is truth, and is no lie, and even as it has taught us, we abide in You.

I say that the lying lips which speak grievous things proudly and contemptuously against us, the righteous men and women, are put to silence. Oh, how great is Your goodness, which You have laid up for us who fear You, which You have wrought for us who trust in You before the sons of men! You hide us in the secret of Your presence from the pride of men: You keep us secretly in a pavilion from the strife of tongues. No weapon that is formed against us shall prosper; and every tongue that rises up against us in judgment we shall condemn. This is the heritage of the servants of the Lord, and our righteousness and holiness is of You.

I thank You, Father, that You watch over Your Word to perform these things in our lives. We walk in confidence that our prayers have been answered because the effectual fervent prayer of a righteous man avails much.

In Jesus' Name, Amen.

Scripture Reference: Eph. 1:17-19; Col. 4:2-4,6; 1:9-13; 1 John 4:17; 1 Cor. 2:16; 1 John 1:3,7; Eph. 4:15; Heb. 4:12; 1 John 2:20,27; Ps. 31:18-20; Is. 54:17; Jer. 1:12 AMP; James 5:16.

A Prophetic Word for Ministries

We have a double portion anointing on us as we flow;
Effectual doors open wherever we go.
Angels are protecting us with great care;
Signs and wonders follow us everywhere.
Favor surrounds us on all sides;
We're walking in meekness and not in pride.
We're on that razor's edge preaching Your word
With great boldness proclaiming what we've heard.
We have wisdom to know and discernment to see;
We are lead by You, Holy Spirit, so totally.
We are financially blessed so abundantly;
We are free from the curse permanently.
We are strengthened in all areas of life;
We are abiding in peace and not in strife.
We have ears to hear and eyes to see;
We're flowing in your perfect will continually.

- by Stephen D. Johnson

4

Confessions

Be it unto me according to thy word.

The Bible way to overcome weakness is by speaking the Word of God in faith. Such confessions of faith, spoken out loud, cause the angels of heaven to hearken to God's Word and to go forth to produce that which was spoken. (Ps. 103:20.) The following are confessions of faith drawn directly from Scripture. Repeat them *daily* to develop strength in every area of your life.

A Confession to Develop Agape Love

I endure long, and am patient and kind; I am never envious nor do I boil over with jealousy; I am not boastful or vainglorious, and I do not display myself haughtily.

I am not conceited—arrogant or inflated with pride; I am not rude (unmannerly), and I do not act unbecomingly. I do not insist on my own rights or my own way, for I am not self-seeking; I am not touchy or fretful or resentful; I take no account of the evil done to me—I pay no attention to a suffered wrong.

I do not rejoice at injustice and unrighteousness, but I rejoice when right and truth prevail.

I bear up under anything and everything that comes, and I am ever ready to believe the best of every person. My hopes are fadeless under all circumstances. I endure everything [without weakening].

I never fail—because love never fails.

GOD IS LOVE.

Scripture Reference: 1 Cor. 13:4-8 AMP; 1 John 4:8

"But I say to you who hear: Love your enemies, do good to those who hate you, bless those who curse you, and pray for those who spitefully use you. To him who strikes you on the one cheek, offer the other also. And from him who takes away your cloak, do not withhold your tunic either. Give to everyone who asks of you. And from him who takes away your goods do not ask them back. And just as you want men to do to you, you also do to them likewise. But if you love those who love you, what credit is that to you? For even sinners love those who love them. And if you do good to those who do good to you, what credit is that to you? For even sinners do the same. And if you lend to those from whom you hope to receive back, what credit is that to you? For even sinners lend to sinners to receive as much back. But love your enemies, do good, and lend, hoping for nothing in return; and your reward will be great, and you will be sons of the Highest. For He is kind to the unthankful and evil. Therefore be merciful, just as your Father also is merciful. Judge not, and you shall not be judged. Condemn not, and you shall not be condemned. Forgive, and you will be forgiven. Give, and it will be given to you: good measure, pressed down, shaken together, and running over will men give unto your bosom. For with the same measure that you use, it will be measured back to you."

Scripture Reference: Luke 6:27-38

I love my enemies; I do good, and I lend hoping for nothing again. My reward is great. I am a child of the Highest for I am kind unto the unthankful and unto the evil. I am merciful as my Father also is merciful. I do not judge, and I am not judged. I do not condemn, and I am not condemned. I forgive, and I am forgiven. I give, and it is given unto me good measure, pressed down, shaken together, and running over, men give unto my bosom; for with the same measure that I mete, it is measured to me again.

Confessions to Overcome Fear

I do not fear; for You are with me: I am not dismayed; for You are my God: You strengthen me; yea, You help me; yea, You uphold me with the right hand of Your righteousness.

Scripture Reference: Is. 41:10

Father, You have not given me a spirit of fear; but of power, and of love, and of a sound mind.

Scripture Reference: 2 Tim. 1:7

Lord, You are on my side; I do not fear: what can man do unto me?

Scripture Reference: Ps. 118:6

I am of You, Father, and have overcome the devil: because greater are You in me, than he that is in the world.

Scripture Reference: 1 John 4:4

Lord, You gave unto me power to tread on serpents and scorpions, and over all the power of the enemy: and nothing by any means hurts me.

Scripture Reference: Luke 10:19

I am the righteousness and holiness of You, Father, because of Jesus. I am far from oppression, fear and

terror, never come near me.

Scripture Reference: 2 Cor. 5:21; Is. 54:14

No weapon that is formed against me prospers; and every tongue that rises against me in judgment I condemn. This is the heritage of the servants of the Lord, and (through Christ) my righteousness is of You, Father.

Scripture Reference: Is. 54:17; 2 Cor. 5:21

Jesus Christ gave Himself for my sins, that He might deliver me from this present evil world, according to the will of God, my Father.

Scripture Reference: Gal. 1:4

There is no evil that befalls me, neither is there any plague or calamity that comes near my (dwelling). For You, Lord, give Your angels [special] charge over me, to accompany and defend and preserve me in all my ways [of obedience and service].

Scripture Reference: Ps. 91:10,11 AMP

I call upon You, Lord, and You always answer me: You are with me in trouble; You deliver me, and honor me. With long life do You satisfy me, and show me Your salvation.

Scripture Reference: Ps. 91:15,16

I Put on The Whole Armor of God

I gird my loins with the truth! Jesus, You are my truth!
Scripture Reference: John 14:16; Ps. 51:6

I put on the breastplate of righteousness. Jesus, You are my righteousness.
Scripture Reference: 2 Cor 5:21

I shod my feet with the preparation of the gospel of peace. Jesus, You are my Peace and readiness!
Scripture Reference: Phil. 4:13

I take the shield of faith, and I quench every fiery dart of the wicked. Jesus, You are the Author and Finisher of my faith.
Scripture Reference: Heb 12:2

I put on the helmet of salvation. Jesus, You are my Salvation.
Scripture Reference: Heb. 5:9

I take the sword of the Spirit (which is the Word of God) to destroy the works of the devil. Jesus, You are my living Word.
Scripture Reference: John 6:63

I pray always in the Spirit. Jesus, You are my baptizer in the Holy Spirit.
Scripture Reference: Matt. 3:11

I now have on the whole armor of God, and I stand against the wiles of the devil. Above all, I take the shield of faith and the sword of the Spirit, and I quench every fiery dart of the wicked. I am always praying with all manner of prayer in the Spirit edifying myself and watching with all perseverance and supplication for all saints.
Scripture Reference: Eph. 6:10-18

I overcome Satan by the blood of the Lamb, and by the word of my testimony.
Scripture Reference: Rev. 12:11

I totally submit myself to You, Father. I resist the devil, and he flees from me.
Scripture Reference: James 4:7

I do not fear; for You, Lord, are with me: I am not dismayed; for You are my God: You strengthen me; and help me; and uphold me with the right hand of Your righteousness.
Scripture Reference: Is. 41:10

O Lord, I magnify You and exalt Your Name every day. I continually seek You, and You deliver me from all my fears. I call unto You, and You hear me, and save me from all my troubles.
Scripture Reference: Ps. 34:3-6

I wait on You, Lord, and You renew my strength; I mount up with wings as eagles; I run, and am not weary; I walk, and do not faint.
Scripture Reference: Is. 40:31

Confessions to Overcome Worry

I do not fret or have any anxiety about anything, because I humble myself under Your mighty hand, Father, that You may exalt me in due time. I cast all my cares upon You, for You care for me. Your peace, which passes all understanding, keeps my heart and mind from worry in Jesus' Name.
Scripture Reference: Phil. 4:6 AMP; 1 Pet. 5:6,7; Phil. 4:7

I continually think on things that are true, honest, *just, pure, lovely, and of a good report.* **I always think** the best *of every person* **and I keep my mind steadfast on all these things.**
Scripture Reference: Phil. 4:8 (Author's paraphrase.)

I am independent of all circumstances.
Scripture Reference: Phil. 4:11 (26 Translations Bible, TCNTN, 20th Century New Testament)

I do all things through You, Lord, who strengthens me.
Scripture Reference: Phil. 4:13

Because I give, it is given unto me; good measure, pressed down, and shaken together, and running over; men give unto my bosom.
Scripture Reference: Luke 6:38

Therefore, I take no thought for my life, what I shall eat, or drink, or wear. Because I seek first the kingdom of God and Your righteousness, all these things are added unto me daily.
Scripture Reference: Matt. 6:25,34

I cast down all imaginations, and every high thing that exalts itself against the knowledge of God, and I bring into captivity every thought to the obedience of Christ.

Scripture Reference: 2 Cor. 10:5

I let Your peace, Father, rule my heart. You keep me in perfect peace, because my mind is stayed on You,

because I trust in You.

Scripture Reference: Col. 3:15; Is. 26:3

Lord, You are the vine, I am the branch. If the root is holy, so are the branches. I am holy, for You are holy.

Scripture Reference: John 15:5; Rom. 11:16; 1 Pet. 1:16.

Confessions for Confidence, Strength and Prosperity

I am that blessed man that does not walk in the counsel of the ungodly, nor do I stand in the way of sinners, nor do I sit in the seat of the scornful. But my delight is in the law of the Lord; and in Your law do I meditate day and night. I am like a tree that is planted by the rivers of water, that brings forth fruit in its season. My leaves do not wither; and whatsoever I do prospers.

Scripture Reference: Ps. 1:1-3

I bless You, Lord, at all times: Your praise is continually in my mouth. My soul makes her boast in You, Lord: I am humble, and I am glad. I magnify You, Lord, and I exalt Your Name. I seek You, Lord, every day. You hear me, and You deliver me from all my fears. I look unto You, and You enlighten me: and I am not ashamed. I cry unto You, Lord, and You hear me, and save me out of all my troubles. The angel of the Lord encamps round about me because I reverence You, and You deliver me. I taste and see that You are good, Lord: I am that blessed man that trusts in You. I fear You, Lord, because I am one of Your saints. I do not have any want because I reverence You. The young lions do lack, and suffer hunger: but I am the one that seeks You, Lord, and I do not want for any good thing.
Scripture Reference: Ps. 34:1-10

I do not forget Your law, Lord; but I let my heart keep Your commandments. Length of days and long life, and peace, they add unto me. I do not forsake mercy or truth: I bind them about my neck; I write them on the tables of my heart. I have favor and good understanding in the sight of You, Father, and all mankind. I trust in You, Lord, with all my heart; I do not lean unto my own understanding. In all my ways I acknowledge You, and You direct my paths. I am not wise in my own eyes; I reverence You and depart from evil. It is health to my nerves ..., and marrow and moistening to my bones. I honor You, Lord, ... with the first fruits of all my income. So my storage places are filled with plenty, and my vats are overflowing with new wine.

Scripture Reference: Prov. 3:1-7; Prov. 3:8-10 AMP

Confessions For Prosperity

Tithing The Tithes

I profess this day unto You, Lord God, that I have come into the inheritance which You, my Lord, has sworn to give me. I am in the land which You have provided for me in Christ Jesus, the Kingdom of Almighty God. I was a sinner serving Satan, he was my god, but I called upon the Name of Jesus, and You heard my cry and delivered me from the power and authority of darkness and translated me into the Kingdom of Your dear Son. Jesus, my Lord and High Priest, I bring the first fruits of my income to You and worship You the Lord my God with it. I rejoice in all the good You have given to me and my household.

I have hearkened to the voice of the Lord my God and have done according to all that You have commanded. Now look down from Your Holy Habitation and bless me as You said in Deuteronomy 26:14, 15 and Malachi 3:10, 11.

Lord, because I am a tither, You open to me the windows of heaven and pour me out such a blessing there is not room enough to receive it. You rebuke the devourer for my sake. You supply all my need according to Your riches in glory by Christ Jesus.
Scripture Reference: Mal. 3:10,11; Phil. 4:19

Lord, You have redeemed me from the curse of the law, being made a curse for me, so that the blessings of Abraham come on me and overtake me. Because I am Christ's, I am Abraham's seed, and an heir according to the promise.
Scripture Reference: Gal. 3:13,14,29; Deut. 28:2

I have caught the thief (Satan). Satan, You must pay me back seven times for everything you have stolen from me, in the Name of the Lord Jesus Christ.
Scripture Reference: John 10:10; Prov. 6:30,31

With You, Father, nothing is impossible. Be it unto me according to Thy Word.
Scripture Reference: Luke 1:37,38

I do not trust in uncertain riches, but in the living God, who gives me richly all things to enjoy. I am rich in good works, always ready to distribute, willing to communicate with everyone.
Scripture Reference: 1 Tim. 6:17,18

I delight myself in You, Lord; and You give me the desires of my heart. I commit my way unto You; I trust also in You; and You bring it to pass.
Scripture Reference: Ps. 37:4,5

Lord, You are my Redeemer, the Holy One of Israel; the Lord my God who teaches me to profit, who leads me in the way that I should go.

Scripture Reference: Is. 48:17

As I deligently listen to the voice of the Lord my God, being careful to do all Your commandments, the Lord my God sets me on high above all the nations of the earth (so that I am not subjected to the flesh in anything).

All these blessings are coming on me and over-taking me as I obey the Lord my God.

I am blessed in the city (my present structure), and I am blessed in the country (my state of expansion).

Blessed is the fruit of my womb and the fruit of my land and the fruit of my soul. I am increasing in my herd (ideas) and in my flock (possessions).

Blessed is my basket (heart) and my kneading bowl (mind).

Blessed am I when I arrive and when I go forth.

The Lord causes my enemies who rise up against me to be defeated before my face. They come out against me one way, and they flee before me seven ways (completely away from me).

The Lord commands blessings upon my barns (all that I have laid up) and in all I put my hand to do, and He blesses me in the land which He gives me.

The Lord establishes me to be holy unto Himself as He promised me, as I keep the commandments of the Lord my God and walk in His ways of light.

All the people of the earth see that I am called by the name of the Lord YHWH (by what He does for me), and they respect me.

The Lord makes me abound in prosperity, in the fruit of my body and in the fruit of my soul and in the fruit of my ground, in the land which the Lord swore to my fathers to give me.

The Lord opens up for me His good storehouses, the heavens, to give rain to my land in its season and to bless all the work of my hand. I am a lender to many nations (people) and not a borrower.

The Lord makes me the head and not the tail. I am above only and not beneath as I listen to the commandments of the Lord my God which I carefully observe. I do not turn aside from any of the words which He commands or orders unto me. I do not serve strange ideas and spirits that are opposed to His orders of life.
Scripture Reference: Deut. 28:1-14

Because I give, it is given unto me; good measure, pressed down, and shaken together, and running over, men give unto my bosom.
Scripture Reference: Luke 6:38

Father, because I give cheerfully and bountifully, You make all grace abound toward me; so that I have all sufficiency in all things, and abound to every good work. You give me seed to sow and then You multiply that seed one hundred fold so that I am enriched in every way to overflowing which causes me to thank You and

praise You all day long.
Scripture Reference: 2 Cor. 9:6-12

Though You were rich, Lord Jesus, for my sake You became poor, that I through Your poverty might be rich.
Scripture Reference: 2 Cor. 8:9

Lord, You are my shepherd; I do not have any want. You supply all my want and need according to Your riches in glory by Christ Jesus.
Scripture Reference: Ps. 23:1; Phil. 4:19

Your blessings, Father, make me rich, and You add no sorrow with it. Since I am the just, the wealth of the sinner is laid up for me.
Scripture Reference: Prov. 10:22; 13:22

I continually give to the poor, therefore I do not lack. Because I walk uprightly, Father, no good thing is withheld from me.
Scripture Reference: Prov. 28:27; Ps. 84:11

Lord, I magnify Your Name, because You take pleasure in the prosperity of Your servant. I do not fear; for it is Your good pleasure to give me the kingdom.
Scripture Reference: Ps. 35:27; Luke 12:32

Lord, You desire above all things that I prosper and be in health, even as my soul prospers.
Scripture Reference: 3 John 2

Father, You have set before me life and death, blessing and cursing: therefore I choose life that both I and my seed live long on the earth.

Scripture Reference: Deut. 30:19,20

I receive Your grace in abundance, and I reign as a king and a priest on the earth.

Scripture Reference: Rom. 5:17; Rev. 1:6

I remember You, the Lord my God: for it is You who gives me power to get wealth, that You may establish Your covenant which You swore unto my fathers, as it is this day.

Scripture Reference: Deut. 8:18

I am willing and obedient and I eat the good of the land.

Scripture Reference: Isaiah 1:19

Confessions for Godly Wisdom and Knowledge

Jesus, You have been made unto me wisdom, righteousness, sanctification and redemption. Therefore I confess that I have Your wisdom, revelation knowledge and understanding living in me to deal wisely in all matters pertaining unto life and godliness. I do all things through You, Jesus, because You strengthen me. Thanks be unto You, Father, You always cause me to triumph in all my affairs of life.

Scripture Reference: 1 Cor. 1:30; 2 Cor. 2:14; 2 Peter 1:3; Phil. 4:13; Col. 1:27, 28

Lord, I let Your Word dwell in me richly in all wisdom. I am filled with the knowledge of Your will in all wisdom and spiritual understanding.

Scripture Reference: Col. 3:16; 1:9

I cast down all imaginations, and every high thing that exalts itself against the knowledge of God, and I bring into captivity every thought to the obedience of Christ.

Scripture Reference: 2 Cor. 10:3-5

Lord Jesus, You are the good shepherd. I know Your voice. A stranger I do not follow, but flee from him: for I do not listen to the voice of strangers.

Scripture Reference: John 10:11,4,5

I present my body a living sacrifice, holy, acceptable unto You, Father, which is my reasonable service. I am not conformed to this world: but I am transformed by the renewing of my mind, that I may prove what is Your good, and acceptable, and perfect, will.

Scripture Reference: Rom. 12:1,2

I humble myself under Your mighty hand, Lord, whereby You exalt me in due time: I cast all my cares upon You; for You care for me.

Scripture Reference: 1 Pet. 5:6,7

Lord, I call unto You, and You always answer me, and show me great and mighty things, which are being revealed to me continually. The manifestation of the Spirit is given to me to profit withal. In Jesus' Name, I claim the word of wisdom, word of knowledge, gift of faith, gifts of healing, working of miracles, gift of prophecy, discerning of spirits,

divers kinds of tongues, and interpretation of tongues. All these are manifested in my life as the Spirit wills.
Scripture Reference: Jer. 33:3; 1 Cor. 12:7-11

I claim all the fruit of the Spirit manifest in my life all the time: agape love, joy, gladness, peace, patience, (an even temper) forbearance, kindness, goodness, (benevolence) faithfulness, gentleness, (meekness, humility) self control, (self restraint) continence. I thank You that all of above are manifest in my life in Jesus' Name!
Scripture Reference: Galatians 5:22-23

I allow no corrupt communication to proceed out of my mouth, but that which is good to edifying, for it ministers grace to the hearers. I do not grieve You, Holy Spirit, whereby I am sealed unto the day of redemption.
Scripture Reference: Eph. 4:29

I speak the truth in love, whereby I grow up unto You, Lord Jesus, in all things. As You are, so am I in this world. I call those things which be not as though they were.
Scripture Reference: Eph. 4:15, 1 John 4:17; Rom. 4:17

Lord, Your joy is my strength. You are the strength of my life.
Scripture Reference: Neh. 8:10; Ps. 27:1

This is the victory that overcomes the world, even my faith. I have overcome the world: because greater are You that is in me, Lord, than he that is in the world.
Scripture Reference: 1 John 4:4,5; 5:4

Lord, I am delivered from the power of darkness, and I am translated into the kingdom of Your dear Son.
Scripture Reference: Col. 1:13

I overcome Satan by the blood of the Lamb, and by the word of my testimony.
Scripture Reference: Rev. 12:11

Confessions for Divine Health

Every sickness, and every disease is under the curse of the law. Lord Jesus, You have redeemed me from the curse of the law, being made a curse for me.
Scripture Reference: Deut. 28:61; Gal. 3:13

Surely, Lord, You have borne my griefs, and carried my sorrows. You were wounded for my transgressions, You were bruised for my iniquities: the chastisement of my peace was upon You; and with Your stripes I am healed.
Scripture Reference: Is. 53:4,5

So that it might be fulfilled which was spoken by the prophet Isaiah, Lord Jesus, You took my infirmities and bore my sicknesses.
Scripture Reference: Matt. 8:17

You, Your own self, bore my sins in Your body on the tree, that I being dead to sins, should live unto righteousness (right standing with the Father): by Your stripes I was healed.
Scripture Reference: 1 Pet. 2:24

I bless You, Lord, O my soul: and all that is within me, I bless Your Holy Name. I bless You, Lord, O my soul, and I do not forget any of Your benefits: You forgive all my iniquities; You heal all my diseases; You redeem my life from destruction; You crown me with loving-kindness and tender mercies; You satisfy my mouth with good things; so that my youth is renewed like the eagle's.
Scripture Reference: Ps. 103:1-5

You sent Your Word, and healed me, and delivered me from all my destructions.
Scripture Reference: Ps. 107:20

I trust in You, Lord, with all my heart; I do not lean unto my own understanding. In all my ways I acknowledge You, and You direct my paths. I am not wise in my own eyes: I reverence You, and depart from evil. It is health and medicine to my nerves and sinews, and marrow and moistening to my bones.
Scripture Reference: Prov. 3:5-7; Prov. 3:8 AMP

I present my body a living sacrifice, holy, acceptable unto You, Lord, which is my reasonable service. Whether therefore I eat, or drink, or whatever I do, I do all for Your glory. For the kingdom of God is not meat and drink; but righteousness, and peace, and joy in the Holy Ghost.
Scripture Reference: Rom. 12:1,2; 1 Cor. 10:31; Rom. 14:17; Mark 11:23

Father, I attend to Your words; I incline my ear unto Your sayings. I do not let them depart from my eyes; I keep them in the midst of my heart. For they are life unto me, and health (medicine) to all my flesh. I keep my heart with all diligence; for out of it are the issues of life.

Scripture Reference: Prov. 4:20-23

For You have restored all health unto me, and have healed me of all my wounds.

Scripture Reference: Jer. 30:17

I serve You, Lord, and You bless my bread, and my water; and You take all sickness away from the midst of me.

Scripture Reference: Ex. 23:25

I give ear to Your commandments, and keep all Your statutes, and You put no disease on me, for You are the Lord who heals me.

Scripture Reference: Ex. 15:26

Therefore You said: Beloved, above all things You want me to prosper and be in health, even as my soul prospers. My soul is my mind, will and emotions. You prosper me spiritually, mentally, physically, socially and financially. So I just thank You that by Your stripes I am healed and made whole and complete.

Scripture Reference: 3 John 2; 1 Pet. 2:24, Ps 103:1

I praise You because I am fearfully and wonderfully made; Your works are wonderful, I know that full well. Therefore every part of my body functions perfectly. Any sickness, disease, germ or pain that touches my body dies instantly!

Scripture Reference: Ps. 139:14 NIV (Author's paraphrase), Mark 11:23

5

The Power and Gifts
of the Holy Spirit

After you have prayed for all the leaders of our great country and other countries, according to 1 Timothy 2:1,2, and have prayed for your loved ones and other people whom God has laid upon your heart, including the fivefold ministries; after you have made the confessions of faith for yourself; then pray as Paul exhorted us in Ephesians 6:18: *Praying always with all prayer and supplication in the Spirit, and watching thereunto with all perseverance and supplication for all saints.*

In this verse Paul is simply saying that we should pray in our own language in agreement with God's Word, and also pray in other tongues.

In Matthew 3:11 John the Baptist said: *I indeed baptize you with water unto repentance: but he that cometh after me is mightier than I, whose shoes I am not worthy to bear: he shall baptize you with the Holy Ghost, and with fire.*

Then in Acts 1:4-8, we read:

And, being assembled together with them, (Jesus) **commanded** *that they* **should not depart** *from Jerusalem, but wait for the promise of the Father, which, saith he, ye have heard of me.*

For John truly baptized with water; but ye shall be baptized with the Holy Ghost not many days hence.

When they therefore were come together, they asked of him, saying, Lord, wilt thou at this time restore again the kingdom to Israel?

And he said unto them, It is not for you to know the times or the seasons, which the Father hath put in his own power.

But ye shall receive power, after that the Holy Ghost is come upon you: and ye shall be witnesses unto me both in Jerusalem, and in all Judaea, and in Samaria, and unto the uttermost part of the earth.

Notice that Jesus said in essence, "You shall receive power, after the Holy Ghost has come upon you: and you shall be witnesses to Me in your own hometown, and in all your own country, and in neighboring countries, and then in the uttermost parts of the earth."

In Acts 2:1-4 we read:

And when the day of Pentecost was fully come, they were all with one accord in one place.

And suddenly there came a sound from heaven as a rushing mighty wind, and it filled all the house where they were sitting.

And there appeared unto them cloven tongues like as of fire, and it sat upon each of them.

And they were all filled with the Holy Ghost, and began to speak with other tongues, as the Spirit gave them utterance.

Let's look further now at Acts 10:38 which tells us *how God anointed Jesus of Nazareth with the Holy Ghost and with power: who went about doing good, and healing all that were oppressed of the devil; for God was with him.*

Notice that God anointed Jesus with the Holy Ghost and power — the same Holy Ghost that John talked about in Matthew 3:11 and the same one Jesus spoke of in Acts 1:8.

Let's go to Acts 10:44-48:

While Peter yet spake these words, the Holy Ghost fell on them which heard the word.

And they of the circumcision which believed were astonished, as many as came with Peter, because that on the Gentiles also was poured out the gift of the Holy Ghost.

For they heard them speak with tongues, and magnify God. Then answered Peter.

Can any man forbid water, that these should not be baptized, which have received the Holy Ghost as well as we?

And he commanded them to be baptized in the name of the Lord. Then prayed they him to tarry certain days.

I would like you to notice that while Peter was preaching about Jesus and the Holy Ghost, the Holy Spirit of which he spoke fell upon the hearers who began to speak with tongues and magnify God.

This incident took place after Peter had received an open vision teaching him that God is no respecter of persons. From this experience he learned that the gift of the Holy Ghost was for the Gentiles as well as for the Jews. These people who heard Peter's message received the baptism of the Holy Ghost by the preaching of the Word of God.

Another way to receive the baptism of the Holy Ghost is recorded in Acts 19:1-6:

And it came to pass, that, while Apollos was at Corinth, Paul having passed through the upper coasts came to Ephesus: and finding certain disciples,

He said unto them, Have ye received the Holy Ghost since ye believed? And they said unto him, We have not so much as heard whether there be any Holy Ghost.

And he said unto them, Unto what then were ye baptized? And they said, Unto John's baptism.

Then said Paul, John verily baptized with the baptism of repentance, saying unto the people, that they should believe on him which should come after him, that is, on Christ Jesus.

When they heard this, they were baptized in the name of the Lord Jesus.

And when Paul had laid his hands upon them, the Holy Ghost came on them; and they spake with other tongues, and prophesied.

In verse 6, after these believers were baptized in water in the name of the Lord Jesus, Paul laid his hands upon them and the Holy Ghost came upon them. They spoke in tongues and prophesied.

In my own case, I personally studied all of these scriptures until I had received revelation knowledge on them. Then I requested prayer that I might receive the baptism in the Holy Ghost. Hands were laid on me and I too began to speak with other tongues, just as these people did.

In Romans 10:17, we are told: *So then faith cometh by hearing, and hearing by the word of God.*

A person cannot have faith until he personally hears and understands what the Spirit of God is saying to him through His Word.

Let's go one step further to explain why believers should speak with other tongues. It's not enough to do something, we need to know why we are doing it. The answer is found in 1 Corinthians 14:1-4:

FOLLOW after charity, and desire spiritual gifts, but rather that ye may prophesy.

For he that speaketh in an unknown tongue speaketh not unto men, but unto God: for no man understandeth him; howbeit in the spirit he speaketh mysteries.

But he that prophesieth speaketh unto men to edification, and exhortation and comfort.

*He that speaketh in an unknown tongue **edifieth himself;** but he that prophesieth edifieth the church.*

The word *edifieth* in the Greek means "to build up."
As a person speaks with other tongues he "builds up"
his inner man (his spirit).

Jude tells us: *But ye, beloved, building up yourselves
on your most holy faith, praying in the Holy Ghost.*

A believer builds himself up by praying in the Holy
Ghost.

There is something else that takes place when one
speaks in tongues:

*For he that speaketh in a unknown tongue speaketh not
unto men, but **unto God:** for no man understandeth him;
howbeit in the spirit he **speaketh mysteries** (1 Cor. 14:2).*

According to Paul, when a person speaks in
tongues he speaks mysteries because he is speaking
directly to God — spirit to Spirit.

You might ask: "If no one will understand what
I'm saying — not even me — why then should I pray
in tongues?"

Don't forget: By speaking in tongues, you are
speaking divine mysteries; you are building up your
spirit man; you are building yourself up on your most
holy faith.

Let's look at what Paul says in 1 Corinthians
14:13-15:

*Wherefore let him that speaketh in an unknown tongue
pray that he may interpret.*

*For if I pray in an unknown tongue, my spirit prayeth,
but my understanding is unfruitful.*

*What is it then? I will pray with the spirit, and I will
pray with the understanding also: I will sing with the spirit,
and I will sing with the understanding also.*

When a person prays in an unknown tongue, his
spirit prays directly to the Father. Since no one else
understands him, he is to pray that he may interpret

what he has been speaking (in the spirit) so they too may be edified (built up).

In John 7:37-39, we read:

In the last day, that great day of the feast, Jesus stood and cried, saying, If any man thirst, let him come unto me, and drink.

He that believeth on me, as the scripture hath said, out of his belly shall flow rivers of living water.

(But this spake he of the Spirit, which they that believe on him should receive: for the Holy Ghost was not yet given; because that Jesus was not yet glorified).

After a person has received the Holy Ghost, out of his "belly" (his spirit) shall flow rivers of living water. When he faces problems that he is unable to handle, he can pray in tongues and draw strength and wisdom from the Spirit of God.

In Romans 8:26-28 Paul tell us:

Likewise the Spirit also helpeth our infirmities: for we know not what we should pray for as we ought: but the Spirit itself maketh intercession for us with groanings which cannot be uttered.

And he that searcheth the hearts knoweth what is the mind of the Spirit, because he maketh intercession for the saints according to the will of God.

And we know that all things work together for good to them that love God, to them who are the called according to his purpose.

In examining thoroughly verse 26, we see that the Spirit helps our "infirmities." This means that when we have a lack of ability to produce results, then the Holy Ghost helps us to solve our problems. When we have done everything we know to do, then we need to pray in the Spirit so He can lead us to receive our answer.

According to Romans 8:27, when we are praying in the Spirit, we are making intercession for the believers (saints) according to the will of God. When we pray in the Spirit, we are praying God's perfect will for our own personal life and that of others. Then and only then will verse 28 be true for us:

And we know that all things work together for good to them that love God, to them who are the called according to his purpose.

Many people have used this scripture to say that everything good or bad works together for their good. I challenge you to study this verse carefully. The more you study it, the more you will know that it applies only to those who are fitting in with God's perfect will. This verse is true only for those who are walking in the Spirit and not in the flesh.

In *The Amplified Bible* version of 1 Corinthians 12:1, we read:

Now about the spiritual gifts (the special endowments of supernatural energy), brethren, I do not want you to be misinformed.

God does not want us to be ignorant of the nine gifts of the Holy Spirit as listed in 1 Corinthians 12:7-11:

*But the manifestation of the Spirit is given to **every man** to profit withal.*

For to one is given by the Spirit the word of wisdom; to another the word of knowledge by the same Spirit;

To another faith by the same Spirit; to another the gifts of healing by the same Spirit;

To another the working of miracles; to another prophecy; to another discerning of spirits; to another divers kinds of tongues; to another the interpretation of tongues.

But all these worketh that one and the selfsame Spirit, dividing to every man severally as he will.

Don't confuse *divers kinds of tongues* and *the interpretation of tongues* with your own personal prayer language (or praying in other tongues). These first two are part of the gifts of the Spirit which are available to every believer when he receives the baptism of the Holy Ghost, but they are given only as the Spirit wills, as we see in verse 11.

I encourage you to study Chapters 12, 13, and 14 of 1 Corinthians. This passage is not everything you need to know pertaining to your prayer language and the nine gifts of the Spirit, but it will enlighten you and encourage you to dig deeper into God's Word.

Paul said in 1 Corinthians 14:18: *I thank my God, I speak with tongues more than ye all.*

That is the reason Paul wrote two-thirds of the New Testament — because he spent hours daily praying in the Spirit. This is how revelation knowledge on the Word of God is received.

Satan has fought against tongues for years. He knows that's where spiritual power and revelation knowledge come from.

In verse 39 of 1 Corinthians 14, Paul writes: *Wherefore, brethren, covet to prophesy, and forbid not to speak with tongues.*

Some people say that tongues are of the devil; some say tongues died with the apostles; some even say that salvation has passed away. Jesus said in Matthew 24:35: *Heaven and earth shall pass away, but my words shall not pass away.*

David writes in Psalm 119:89: *For ever, O Lord, thy word is settled in heaven.*

In Psalm 138:2 he states that God has magnified His Word above His name.

In Philippians 2:9 Paul declares that God has given His Son Jesus a Name above EVERY name.

Therefore, after examining the last few verses, how can anyone say that any scripture has been done away with?

Finally, in Hebrews 4:1,2, we read:

Let us therefore fear, lest, a promise being left us of entering into his rest, any of you should seem to come short of it.

For unto us was the gospel preached, as well as unto them: but the word preached did not profit them, not being mixed with faith in them that heard it.

Translated, the last two scriptures mean that as we hear the Word of God, we either believe it or we don't. If we do believe it — if it is mixed with faith — that Word will profit us.

In order to profit from the Word of God, a person must have faith. But faith is not merely believing. Faith demands action. James tells us: *But be ye doers of the word, and not hearers only, deceiving your own selves.*

Tongues are given to believers to help us in our daily walk. We are to be victorious Christians, fighting the good fight of faith. The prophet Isaiah says of the Lord:

For with stammering lips and another tongue will he speak to this people.

To whom he said, This is the rest wherewith ye may cause the weary to rest; and this is the refreshing: yet they would not hear (Is. 28:11,12).

In Hebrews 4:11 we are told: *Let us labour therefore to enter into that rest, lest any man fall after the same example of unbelief.*

I trust that this book has enlightened you on the power of God's Word, the power of the baptism of the Holy Spirit, and the purpose and power of praying in tongues. Just a lasting reminder: Faith is believing God! Believing God is simply acting on what He has said in His Word!

That kind of believing action is the God-kind of faith which will bring total prosperity in life with Jesus Christ.

A Prayer for Salvation

Pray this prayer out loud with me right now.

Father, I come to You in Jesus' Name. I thank You for the word in this book. I thank You that You said in Romans 10:9-10 that if I would confess with my mouth and believe in my heart that God raised Jesus from the dead that I would be saved. Come into my heart and make me a brand new creature. And I confess it with my mouth. Jesus, You are my Lord and I believe in my heart that God raised You from the dead. I am now saved. I ask You to forgive me of all of my sins. I confess all of my past sins, and I thank You, Father, for forgiving me. I also read that You want me filled with the Holy Spirit. So I ask You now to fill me from the top of my head to the soles of my feet with the Holy Spirit. Thank You, Father for saving me and filling me with the Holy Spirit. And I thank You, Lord, according to Your Word now I am the righteousness of God. I am holy because You are holy. I am saved and filled with Your Spirit, set apart ready for the Masters use. Amen.

References

Unless otherwise indicated, all Scripture quotations are taken from the *King James Version* of the Bible.

Some Scripture quotations marked *AMP* are taken from *The Amplified Bible, New Testament*. Copyright © 1954, 1958 by the Lockman Foundation, La Habra, California.

Some Scripture quotations marked *AMP* are taken from *The Amplified Bible, Old Testament*. Copyright © 1962, 1964 by Zondervan Publishing House, Grand Rapids, Michigan.

Verses marked *TLB* are taken from *The Living Bible*. Copyright © 1971 by Tyndale House Publishers, Wheaton, Illinois.

Scripture quotations marked *NIV* are taken from *The Holy Bible: New International Version*. Copyright © 1978 by the New York International Bible Society. Used by permission of Zondervan Bible Publishers.

Some Scripture quotations are taken from the new KJV of the Bible. Some quotations are combinations of the above.